Primary Maths for Scotland

1st Level Maths
Textbook 1C

Series Editor: Craig Lowther

Authors: Antoinette Irwin, Carol Lyon,
Kirsten Mackay, Felicity Martin, Scott Morrow

© 2019 Leckie & Leckie Ltd

001/31052019

10 9 8 7 6 5 4 3

ISBN 9780008313975

Published by
Leckie & Leckie Ltd
An imprint of HarperCollins*Publishers*
Westerhill Road, Bishopbriggs, Glasgow, G64 2QT
T: 0844 576 8126   F: 0844 576 8131
leckieandleckie@harpercollins.co.uk   www.leckieandleckie.co.uk

Publisher: Fiona McGlade
Managing editor: Craig Balfour
Project editors: Alison James and Peter Dennis

Special thanks
Answer checking: Caleb O'Loan
Copy editing: Louise Robb
Cover design: Ink Tank
Layout and illustration: Jouve
Proofreading: Dylan Hamilton

A CIP Catalogue record for this book is available from the British Library.

Acknowledgements

Images © Shutterstock.com

Printed in Italy by GRAFICA VENETA S.p.A.

Contents

Answers and free downloadable resources

Answers

All answers to the Before we start, Let's practise and Challenge questions in Textbooks 1A, 1B and 1C can be downloaded from our website here:

https://collins.co.uk/primarymathsforscotland

Free downloadable resources

There are free downloadable resources to support Textbooks 1A, 1B and 1C. These can be downloaded, printed out and photocopied for in-class use from our website here:

https://collins.co.uk/primarymathsforscotland

There are two types of resources:

- **General resources.** These are helpful documents that can be used alongside Textbooks 1A, 1B and 1C, and include, for example, blank ten frames, number lines, 100 squares and blank clock faces.

- **Specific resources.** These are supporting worksheets that relate to either a particular area of learning or a specific question and are labelled with a unique resource reference number. For example, 'Resource1C_7.1_Let's_practise_Q2' is a specific downloadable resource for Textbook 1C, Chapter 7.1, Let's practise Question 2.

1.1 Rounding

> We are learning to round numbers to the nearest hundred.

Before we start

Put these numbers in order from smallest to biggest.

| 600 | 800 | 500 | 700 |

> We can use number lines to help us round up or down.

Let's learn

We can use a number line to help us round numbers to the nearest hundred.

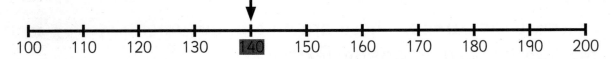

100 110 120 130 **140** 150 160 170 180 190 200

The number 140 is between 100 and 200, but it is closer to the number 100, so we round **down**.

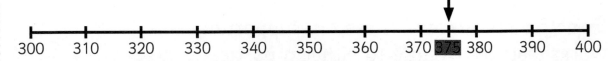

300 310 320 330 340 350 360 370 **375** 380 390 400

The number 375 is between 300 and 400, but it is closer to the number 400, so we round **up**.

If a number ends in 50, we usually round **up**.

0 10 20 30 40 **50** 60 70 80 90 100

1) Which is the closest hundred to these numbers?

Use the number lines to help you.

a) 337

300 310 320 330 340 350 360 370 380 390 400

b) 458

400 410 420 430 440 450 460 470 480 490 500

c) 514

500 510 520 530 540 550 560 570 580 590 600

d) 891

800 810 820 830 840 850 860 870 880 890 900

2) Round these numbers to the nearest hundred:

a) 914   b) 550   c) 82   d) 463   e) 989

3) Copy and complete the table in your jotter.

Cars made	Sunday	Monday	Tuesday	Wednesday
Actual number	362	275	188	221
Rounded to nearest 10	360	?	?	?
Rounded to nearest 100	?	?	?	?

CHALLENGE!

a) Amman thinks of a number. Rounded to the nearest ten it is 450. Rounded to the nearest hundred it is 400. It is an even number.

What are all the possible numbers he could have started with?

b) Nuria is thinking of a number. If she rounds it to the nearest hundred it would be a four-digit number. If she rounds it to the nearest ten it would be 950.

What are all the possible numbers she could have started with?

c) Make up some more rounding puzzles for a partner to solve.

1.2 Estimating the answer by rounding

We are learning to estimate by rounding and comparing the answer with the estimate.

Before we start

a) What is this number rounded to the nearest hundred?

b) What number is 100 more than this number?

824

We can use rounding to estimate whether an answer is correct.

Let's learn

We can round numbers to the nearest ten or hundred to help us estimate whether an answer is correct.

Nuria and Finlay have worked out the answer to 338 − 159.

Nuria's answer is 279. Finlay's answer is 179.

We can use rounding to estimate which answer is more likely to be correct.

338 rounded to the nearest hundred is 300.

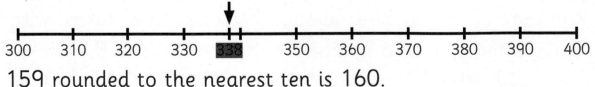

159 rounded to the nearest ten is 160.

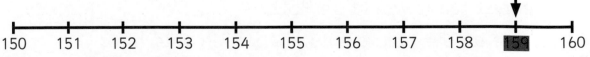

300 − 160 = 140 so we can estimate that Finlay's answer of 179 is more likely to be correct.

1) Read these number problems. Use rounding to estimate the answers and check which ones are reasonable. Give a new estimate to any that are unreasonable.
   a) 57 + 27 is about 714.
   b) 51 + 28 is about 80.
   c) 139 + 18 is about 220.
   d) 18 + 48 is about 516.
   e) 27 + 68 is about 100.
   f) 48 + 97 is about 200.

2) Read these number problems. Use rounding to estimate the answers and check which ones are reasonable. Give a new estimate to any that are unreasonable.
   a) 138 − 29 is about 110.
   b) 76 − 38 is less than 20.
   c) 178 − 18 − 9 is about 120.
   d) 97 − 51 is close to 100.
   e) 98 − 21 is less than 50.
   f) 96 − 69 is close to 0.

3) Isla has worked out the answers to these problems. Estimate the answer to these problems by rounding to the nearest ten, then compare Isla's answers with your estimates.
   Are her answers reasonable?
   a) 118 + 103 = 221
   b) 903 − 149 = 952
   c) 296 + 211 = 507
   d) 862 − 59 = 353

⭐ **CHALLENGE!** ....

For the calculations below, Isla estimated that the number of cookies she had sold was as follows:
a) Number of cinnamon cookies sold = 403 − 169.
   Isla's estimate is 130.
   Is her estimate reasonable? If not, what is your estimate?
b) Number of ginger cookies sold = 399 − 151.
   Isla's estimate is 200.
   Is her estimate reasonable? If not, what is your estimate?

2 Number – order and place value

2.1 Recognising and writing three-digit numbers

> We are learning to recognise and write three-digit numbers.

Before we start

Look at this three-digit number.

a) Write this number in words.

b) Now write this number backwards in numerals.

c) Can you write this new number in words too?

459

> We can write three-digit numbers in numerals and in words.

Let's learn

This place value house shows the number 218.

In numerals: **218**.

In words: **two hundred and eighteen**.

218 is made up of **2** hundreds, **1** ten and **8** ones.

H	T	O
2	1	8

> Don't forget to write **and** after the word 'hundred'.

1) Write the number shown by each place value house in numerals and in words.

a)
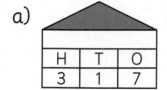

H	T	O
3	1	7

b)

H	T	O
4	2	4

c)
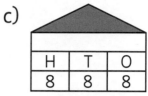

H	T	O
8	8	8

d)
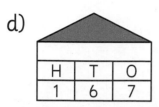

H	T	O
1	6	7

e)
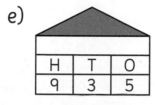

H	T	O
9	3	5

f)
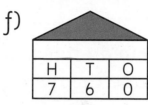

H	T	O
7	6	0

2) a) Which colour card shows the number made with:
   i)   7 hundreds, 2 tens and 1 one
   ii) 8 hundreds, 5 tens and 6 ones
   iii) 2 hundreds, 3 tens and 0 ones

   b) Which card is left over?
   Draw a place value house to show this number.

eight hundred and fifty-six   nine hundred and eleven

two hundred and thirty   seven hundred and twenty-one

⭐ CHALLENGE! ....

How many different three-digit numbers can you make with these digit cards? Write each number you make in numerals and in words.

 3   0   5

2.2 Zero as a place holder

We are learning to use zero correctly when reading and writing three-digit numbers.

Before we start

Amman thinks he has made the number **207**.

a) Explain why he is wrong.

b) Write the number Amman has made in numerals and in words.

Three-digit numbers are made up of hundreds, tens and ones.

Let's learn

350 is a three-digit number.

It is made up of 3 hundreds, 5 tens and 0 ones.

The 3 has a value of three hundred. The 5 has a value of fifty. The 0 has a value of zero.

Zero is the place holder. It keeps the hundreds and tens digits in place.

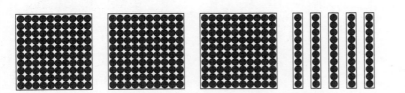

H	T	O
3	5	0

406 is a three-digit number.

It is made up of 4 hundreds, 0 tens and 6 ones.

The 4 has a value of four hundred. The 0 has a value of zero. The 6 has a value of 6.

Zero is the place holder. It keeps the hundreds and ones digits in place.

H	T	O
4	0	6

1) Write the number shown by each place value house in numerals and in words.

a)

H	T	O
7	0	3

b)

H	T	O
6	1	0

c)

H	T	O
8	0	5

d)

H	T	O
4	0	4

e)

H	T	O
4	4	0

f)

H	T	O
9	0	2

g)

H	T	O
2	9	0

h)

H	T	O
1	0	4

i)

H	T	O
5	0	5

j)

H	T	O
5	5	0

k)

H	T	O
3	0	1

l)

H	T	O
9	7	0

2) Write these numbers in numerals and describe the position of the place holder. One has been done for you.

    a) three hundred and eight   **308**   **The place holder is in the tens position.**
    b) two hundred and two
    c) four hundred and ninety
    d) five hundred and twenty
    e) one hundred and one
    f) one hundred and eighty
    g) seven hundred and ten
    h) six hundred

3) Use these digit cards to make up as many three-digit numbers as you can.   **7 0 2**

Explain the value of zero in each of your numbers.

CHALLENGE!

Mrs Wallace calls out a number and asks the children to write it in numerals.

> nine hundred and one

a) Isla writes 9001.
   Explain why Isla is wrong.

b) Finlay writes 910.
   Explain why Finlay is wrong.

c) Write what Isla and Finlay should have written.

2 | Number – order and place value

2.3 Number sequences (1)

We are learning to count forwards and backwards in 1s, 10s and 100s.

Before we start

Isla is counting down the days to her holiday.
Continue Isla's chart.

303 days to go!	302 days to go!	301 days to go!	? days to go!	? days to go!	? days to go!

Number patterns and place value can help us to read, write and order numbers correctly.

Let's learn

99 is the largest whole number with two digits.
It has **9 tens and 9 ones**.

T	O
9	9

The number after 99 is 100.
The number **100** has **1 hundred**, **0 tens and 0 ones**.

H	T	O
1	0	0

Ten more than 99 is 109.
The number **109** has **1 hundred**,
0 tens and 9 ones.

Ten more than 100 is 110.
The number **110** has **1 hundred**,
1 ten and 0 ones.

One hundred more than 99 is 199.
The number **199** has **1 hundred**,
9 tens and 9 ones.

One hundred more than 199 is 299.
The number **299** has **2 hundreds**,
9 tens and 9 ones.

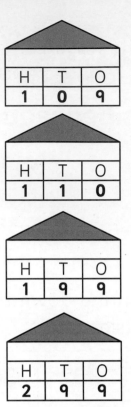

H	T	O
1	0	9

H	T	O
1	1	0

H	T	O
1	9	9

H	T	O
2	9	9

Let's practise

1) a) Start at number 401. Count backwards from there by
   ones. Write down a number for each empty box.

401	?	?	?	?	?	?	?	?

   Now try this with 301, 201 and 101.

   b)
301	?	?	?	?	?	?	?	?

   c)
201	?	?	?	?	?	?	?	?

   d)
101	?	?	?	?	?	?	?	?

   Use a number line to check your answers.
   Talk with a partner about what you notice.

2) Write the numbers that are 10 more **and** 100 more than:
   a) 475   b) 297   c) 501   d) 793

3) Write the numbers that are 10 less **and** 100 less than:
   a) 182   b) 608   c) 300   d) 808

4) Complete the following number sequences in your jotter.

   a) 546, 556, ? , ? , ? , ? , ? , ?

   b) 208, 308, ? , ? , ? , ? , ? , ?

   c) 332, 322, ? , ? , ? , ? , ? , ?

   d) 707, 607, ? , ? , ? , ? , ? , ?

CHALLENGE!

Use the clues to work out Finlay's mystery three-digit number.

> My number is even.
> It sits in-between 800 and 900 on the number line.
> The sum of its digits is 18.
> It is 10 more than 872 and 100 less than 982.

Think of a different three-digit number and write some clues.
Can your partner guess your mystery number?

2 Number – order and place value

2.4 Number sequences (2)

> We are learning to skip count forwards in 20s, 25s and 50s.

Before we start

How many bugs altogether? Explain how you worked it out.

> Number patterns and place value can help us count in 20s, 25s and 50s.

Let's learn

Talk about what you see. Can you continue each sequence?

20 books in each box

| 20 | 40 | 60 | 80 | 100 | 120 |

There are **120** books altogether.

50 sweets in each jar

| 50 | 100 | 150 | 200 | 250 | 300 | 350 | 400 | 450 |

There are **450** sweets altogether.

25 apples in each crate

| 25 | 50 | 75 | 100 | 125 | 150 |

There are **150** apples altogether.

1) Complete the sequences by skip counting across the planets to get to the rockets. Write your answers in your jotter.

a)

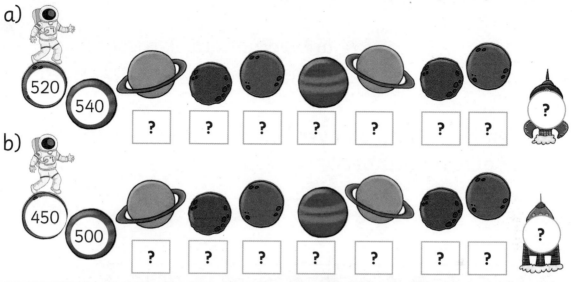

520 540 ? ? ? ? ? ? ? ?

b)

450 500 ? ? ? ? ? ? ? ?

2) Skip count forwards in 25s to fill in the numbers on the parcels. Write your answers in your jotter.

a) 125 ? ? ? ? ? ?

b) 350 ? ? ? ? ? ?

⭐ CHALLENGE!

Play Skip Count Ping Pong with a partner. Start at **10** and take turns to skip count forwards in **20s**. How far can you go?

2.5 Number sequences (3)

We are learning to skip count backwards in 20s, 25s and 50s.

Before we start

Nuria's pen has leaked all over her work!
Write the missing numbers.

a)

64 66 70 82 84

b)

90 130 135 140 145 150

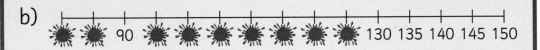

Number patterns and place value can help us count in 20s, 25s and 50s.

Let's learn

Start at the top and read **down** each ladder.
Talk about what you notice.
Can you continue each pattern down to zero?

140	350	200
120	300	175
100	250	150
80	200	125
60	150	100

1) Copy and complete each number sequence.

a) ▲? ▲? ▲? ▲? ▲? ▲300 ▲350

b) ▭? ▭? ▭? ▭? ▭? ▭425 ▭450

c) ⬭? ⬭? ⬭? ⬭? ⬭850 ⬭900 ⬭?

d) ★? ★? ★? ★65 ★85 ★? ★?

e) ◆? ◆? ◆? ◆? ◆230 ◆280 ◆?

Number lines

CHALLENGE! ....

Use an empty number line for each question.
Start at **800** each time and skip count backwards.
Say and write the numbers you land on.

a) How many jumps of 20 to reach 700?

b) How many jumps of 25 to reach 700?

c) How many jumps of 50 to reach 700?

d) If you keep skip counting backwards from 700 in jumps of 20, 25 and 50, what is the next number that you will write on each of your number lines?

2 Number – order and place value

2.6 Representing and describing three-digit numbers

> We are learning to build and describe three-digit numbers.

Before we start

Which is the odd one out? Justify your answer.

a)

b)

c)

d) twenty-one

e)

f)

g)

> The position of each digit tells us its value.

Let's learn

From left to right, three-digit numbers have values of hundreds (100s), tens (10s) and ones (1s).

The same digit can have different values. For example, in the number 148 the 4 is worth four tens (40) but in the number 481 the 4 is worth four hundreds (400).

We can use base 10 material to build three-digit numbers.

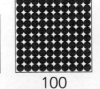
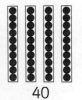

100   40   8

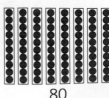

400   80   1

1) Write each number shown using numerals and in words.

a)

b)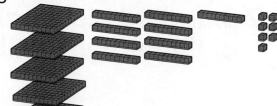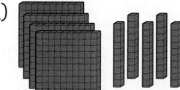

c)

d)

2) In the number 716, the value of the 7 is seven hundreds or 700. Write the value of the 7 in these numbers in both words and numerals.

a) 372   b) 117   c) 570   d) 789   e) 997   f) 784

3) Work with a partner. Represent each number using dot squares and strips or base 10 blocks. Draw what you made.

a) 229   b) 306   c) 114   d) 510   e) 800   f) 209

CHALLENGE!

a) Amman wrote a three-digit number. He put an 8 in the ones place, a 5 in the tens place and a 1 in the hundreds place. Write down Amman's number.

b) Amman then took away one hundred and added ten. What number does he have now?

2.7 Standard place value partitioning of three-digit numbers

> We are learning to partition three-digit numbers into hundreds, tens and ones.

Before we start

These blocks show a three-digit number.

a) What number is it?

b) Show the number in another way using different equipment.

> We can **partition** three-digit numbers into hundreds, tens and ones.

Let's learn

Let's partition 675.

6 is in the hundreds place. Its value is **600**.

7 is in the tens place. Its value is **70**.

5 is in the ones place. Its value is **5**.

600 + 70 + 5 = 675

H	T	O
6	7	5

We can make the number 675 with place value arrow cards.

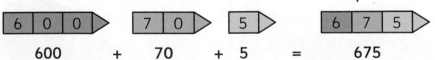

675

We can make the number 675 with place value counters.

600   +   70   +   5   =   675

1) What numbers do the arrow cards show? Write down each number in your jotter. One has been done for you.

   a) | 2 | 0 | 0 | | 8 | 0 | | 4 | = 284

   b) | 1 | 0 | 0 | | 6 | 0 | | 7 | = ?

   c) | 4 | 0 | 0 | | 8 | 0 | | 2 | = ?

   d) | 2 | 0 | 0 | | 7 | 0 | | 9 | = ?

   e) | 3 | 0 | 0 | | 2 | 0 | | 8 | = ?

   f) | 4 | 0 | 0 | | 2 | 0 | | 5 | = ?

2) Make these numbers with place value arrow cards. Draw the place value arrow cards you use each time.

   a) 837   b) 551   c) 374   d) 993

   e) 688   f) 726   g) 914   h) 749

3) We can represent three-digit numbers with base 10 blocks.

   159 = 100 + 50 + 9

   In your jotter, write the number represented by each set of base 10 blocks then partition it into hundreds, tens and ones.

   a)

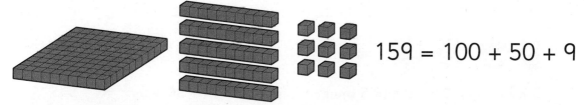

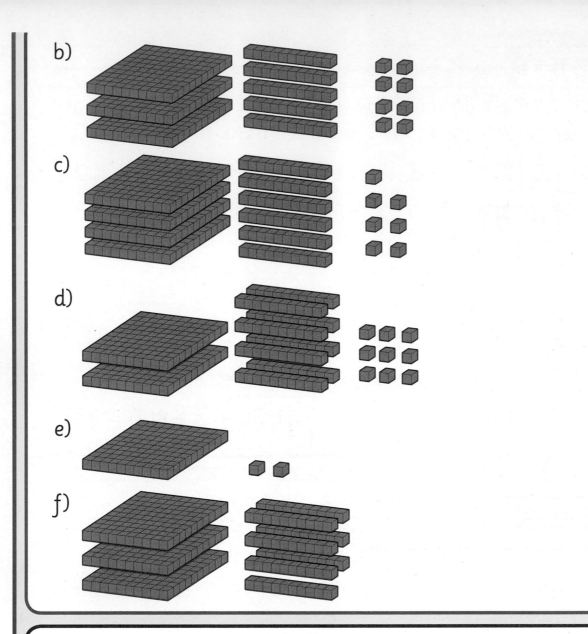

b)

c)

d)

e)

f)

4) Write the total represented by each set of place value counters in two different ways. One has been done for you.

a) 100 100 100 100 100 10 10 10 1 1 1 1 1

   5 hundreds, 3 tens and 5 ones   =   **500 + 30 + 5**   =   **535**

b) 100 100 100 100 100 100 10 1 1 1 1

c) 100 100 100 100 100 100 100 1

d) 100 100 100 100 100 100 100 100 10 10

5) Write the numbers that have been partitioned into hundreds, tens and ones.

a) 300   70   2   b) 3   900   10

c) 100   20   9   d) 70   6   200

e) 700   5   30   f) 7   40   400

6) True or false?

a) 80 + 3 + 300 = 338   b) 2 + 40 + 400 = 244

c) 9 + 50 + 100 = 159   d) 600 + 40 + 1 = 614

e) 800 + 10 + 4 = 814   f) 30 + 2 + 400 = 432

CHALLENGE!

a) Here are some arrow cards.
   Use them to make as many different three-digit numbers as you can.

| 4 | 0 | 0 | | 2 | 0 | | 5 |

| 9 | | 3 | 0 | 0 | | 7 | 0 |

b) Is it possible to make a three-digit number using only **two** place value arrow cards? Explain.

c) How many three-digit numbers between 100 and 200 can be made using only two place value arrow cards each time? Make a list.

2.8 Non-standard place value partitioning of two-digit numbers

> We are learning to partition two-digit numbers in different ways.

Before we start

Can you explain what each of these digits is worth and which is the biggest in value? If it helps, you can use arrow cards to make the number first.

a) 489   4 is worth?

b) 489   8 is worth?

c) 489   9 is worth?

d) The digit with the biggest value is [?] because [?].

> A number can be partitioned in many different ways.

Let's learn

Let's partition the number 75 in different ways.

70 + 5 = 75

60 + 15 = 75

50 + 25 = 75

How else could you partition 75 into tens and ones?

1) Isla uses place value counters. She partitions the number 32 in three different ways.

Being able to partition numbers into tens and ones helps us to add and subtract mentally.

30 + 2 = 32

20 + 12 = 32

10 + 22 = 32

Partition each number into tens and ones in **at least four different ways**. You may use base 10 blocks or place value counters to help you.

a) 81   b) 49   c) 93   d) 54   e) 68   f) 76

2) Find the missing number. One has been done for you.

a)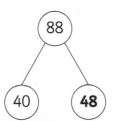

b)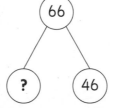

c)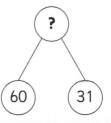

CHALLENGE!

The number **234** can be partitioned into **200 + 30 + 4**. How many other ways can you find to partition 234 into hundreds, tens and ones? Write them down.

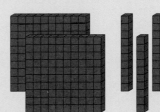

2.9 Comparing two- and three-digit numbers

We are learning to compare numbers.

Before we start

Look at this three-digit number.

624

a) Write this number in words.

b) Write a three-digit number, in numerals and words, that is greater than this number.

c) Write a three-digit number, in numerals and words, that is less than this number.

When comparing numbers, we need to think about the **value** of the digits.

Let's learn

As mathematicians, we can use symbols to compare the size of numbers and amounts:

< means 'is less than'   > means 'is more than'
≠ means 'does not equal'

Let's compare the numbers 38 and 380.

In the number **3**8, the 3 has a value of **30**.

In the number **3**80, the 3 has a value of **300**.

38 is less than 380 and 380 is greater than 38.

38 < 380 and **380 > 38**   **38 ≠ 380**

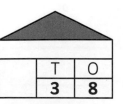

If the first digit of each number has the same value, we need to look at the second digit to work out which is greater and which is less.

1) True or false?

   a) 438 is greater than 432
   b) 101 is greater than 110
   c) 77 is equal to 707
   d) 900 is less than 909

2) Nuria has made these numbers out of digit cards.
   Can you rearrange each set of digit cards to make a number that makes the statement true?

   For example: 4 8 7 < 7 8 4

   a)   ? ? ?

   b)   ? ? ?

   c)   ? ? ?

3) Finlay is trying to work out how to make this number statement correct. Write down three different ways he could do this. You may only change a number **or** a symbol each time.

   357 = 375 ✗

Use the numbers on these cards to make each number statement true. How many different ways can you find?

51   510   501   ? > ?   ? < ?   ? ≠ ?

2.10 Ordering two- and three-digit numbers

Before we start

We are learning to order numbers.

Correct Amman's work. For each wrong answer, write what Amman should have written.

a) 578 > 785   b) 202 = 220   c) 491 > 149
d) 659 < 695   e) 150 < 105   f) 083 ≠ 83

When ordering numbers, we need to think about the **value** of the digits.

Let's learn

Let's order these numbers from smallest to largest.

173   127   79   179   197

There is one two-digit number and four three-digit numbers. Two-digit whole numbers are smaller than three-digit whole numbers so **79 is the smallest number**.

All of the three-digit numbers have 1 hundred. We need to look at the tens digit to work out which number comes next.
127 has 2 tens. 173 and 179 both have 7 tens. 197 has 9 tens.

127 is the second smallest number and **197 is the largest number**.

173 is smaller than 179.

The correct order is: **79   127   173   179   197**

We can check our answer on an empty number line.

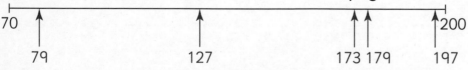

1) Write each set of numbers in order from smallest to largest. Check your answers by drawing an empty number line.

Number lines

   a) 156, 175, 149, 132, 160   b) 230, 320, 132, 231, 131

   c) 475, 457, 405, 500, 499   d) 928, 916, 924, 918, 91

2) a) Miss Black asks Finlay to order these numbers from largest to smallest.

   526   521   59   50   508   540   567   518

   Finlay thinks that 59 is the largest number because the second digit is 9, which is bigger than 2, 0, 4, 6 and 1. Explain why Finlay is incorrect.

   b) Write the numbers in the correct order from largest to smallest.

3) Now write these sets of numbers in order from largest to smallest. Check your answers by drawing an empty number line.

   a) 424, 321, 231, 412, 421   b) 634, 628, 617, 671, 638

   c) 838, 858, 383, 833, 358   d) 119, 112, 121, 19, 11

⭐ CHALLENGE!

Work with a partner. Use these digit cards to make as many two-digit **and** three-digit numbers as you can. You may use each digit only once each time. For example, you can make the number 301 but not the number 303.

7 3 1 0 5

Can you write the numbers you have made in order from smallest to largest?

2 Number – order and place value

2.11 Ordinal numbers

We are learning to use words to describe the order of people, objects or events.

Before we start

Isla was born on the twenty-fifth of February.
We can write 'twenty-fifth' in symbols: **25th**
Write these birth dates using symbols:

a) Nuria: thirtieth of July   b) Amman: twenty-third of March
c) Finlay: thirty-first of May   d) Isla's dog: twenty-second of June

Ordinal numbers describe the position of people, objects or events.

Let's learn

Most ordinal numbers end with the letters **th**. For example:
Finlay's mum came **fifty-eighth** (**58th**) in the marathon.
Some ordinal numbers end with the letters **st**. For example:
Isla was on the **seventy-first** (**71st**) page of her book.
Some ordinal numbers end with the letters **nd**. For example:
Amman's mum was **thirty-second** (**32nd**) in the ticket-queue.
Some ordinal numbers end with the letters **rd**. For example:
Nuria's gran has just had her **sixty-third** (**63rd**) birthday.

1) Match each ordinal number with a card colour.
   a) forty-second – pink
   b) eighty-seventh
   c) three hundred and first
   d) five hundred and twelfth
   e) Which card doesn't have a partner? Write this ordinal number in words.

301st	72nd	87th	42nd	512th

2) Write these ordinal numbers in words.
   a) 145th   b) 82nd   c) 61st

3) The planes are queueing for take-off. The plane at the front of the queue will be the 39th plane to leave the airport today. Write the position of the next five planes in words and symbols.

CHALLENGE!

a) Isla's grandpa lives on the 26th floor. Mrs Smith lives five floors below him. What floor does Mrs Smith live on? Write your answer in words and symbols.

b) Amman is on the 142nd page of his book. If he reads 10 more pages, what page will he be on? Write your answer in words and symbols.

3.1 Adding and subtracting a one-digit number to and from a three-digit number

Bara

We are learning to use number bonds and place value to add and subtract.

Before we start

Complete these subtraction number statements.
The first one has been done for you.

a)

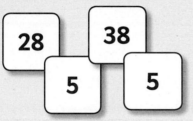

| 28 | – | 5 | = | 23 |

| 38 | – | 5 | = | 33 |

b)

| ? | – | ? | = | ? |

| ? | – | ? | = | ? |

c)

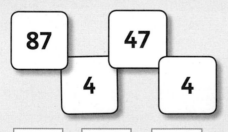

| ? | – | ? | = | ? |

| ? | – | ? | = | ? |

d)

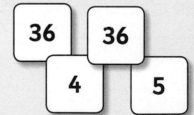

| ? | – | ? | = | ? |

| ? | – | ? | = | ? |

We can use number bonds and place value to help us with addition and subtraction.

Ellie

The girls are working out the answer to **7 + 146**.

They know that 7 + 146 = **146 + 7**.

I partitioned 7 into 4 and 3.
146 + **4** = 150 → 150 + **3** = 153
The answer is 153.

6 + 7 = 13
140 + 13 = 153
The answer is 153.

 Ellie

 Nina

Talk about the girls' strategies. Which strategy do you prefer?

How would you calculate 239 – 5? What about 321 – 8?

Let's practise

1) Use addition facts and place value to help you answer each set of questions. Write your answers in your jotter.

   a)   4 + 3 = ?   b)   6 + 6 = ?   c)   5 + 8 = ?

      114 + 3 = ?   106 + 6 = ?   125 + 8 = ?

      134 + 3 = ?   306 + 6 = ?   145 + 8 = ?

      154 + 3 = ?   506 + 6 = ?   165 + 8 = ?

      194 + 3 = ?   706 + 6 = ?   185 + 8 = ?

2) Use subtraction facts and place value to help you answer each set of questions. Write your answers in your jotter.

   a)   8 – 2 = ?   b)   14 – 7 = ?   c)   12 – 7 = ?

      108 – 2 = ?   314 – 7 = ?   112 – 7 = ?

128 – 2 = ?   514 – 7 = ?   122 – 7 = ?

148 – 2 = ?   714 – 7 = ?   132 – 7 = ?

168 – 2 = ?   914 – 7 = ?   142 – 7 = ?

3) Copy and complete these additions in your jotter.

    a) 483 + 5 = ?   b) 281 + 7 = ?   c) 736 + 4 = ?

    d) 396 + 5 = ?   e) 119 + 5 = ?   f) 597 + 6 = ?

4) Copy and complete these subtractions in your jotter.

    a) 329 – 8 = ?   b) 678 – 6 = ?   c) 844 – 4 = ?

    d) 277 – 9 = ?   e) 435 – 7 = ?   f) 501 – 2 = ?

CHALLENGE!

How many different ways can you find to make each number sentence true? List them.

a) 3 ? 7 + ? = 3 ? 1

b) 1 ? 3 – ? = 1 ? 8

3.2 Adding and subtracting 10 and 100

We are learning to add or subtract 10 or 100 to or from a three-digit number.

Before we start

Finlay guesses that there are 198 sweets in the jar.

Nuria thinks there are 100 less than 198.

Isla thinks there are 10 more than 198.

a) How many sweets does Nuria think there are?

b) How many sweets does Isla think there are?

We can use place value to help us to add and subtract.

Let's learn

Isla makes the number 352 with base 10 blocks. She shows her number on a place value house.

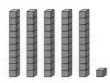

H	T	O
3	5	2

She adds 100 to her number **352 + 100 = 452**

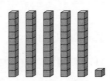

H	T	O
4	5	2

Then she subtracts 10 from the new number she has made.
452 − 10 = 442

H	T	O
4	4	2

Let's practise

1) Add 10 to each number.
   a) 675   b) 709   c) 242   d) 515   e) 981   f) 498

2) Add 100 to each number.
   a) 366   b) 101   c) 280   d) 817   e) 411   f) 69

3) Subtract 10 from each number.
   a) 454   b) 512   c) 399   d) 700   e) 902   f) 105

4) Subtract 100 from each number.
   a) 888   b) 303   c) 720   d) 519   e) 660   f) 108

5) Find the missing number. Write your answers in your jotter.

   a) [?] + 45 = 545   b) 808 + [?] = 818

   c) 900 = [?] + 800   d) 356 − [?] = 326

   e) 490 = [?] − 10   f) 204 = 100 + [?]

CHALLENGE!

Prove why Amman is wrong. How many three-digit numbers **do** have zero in the 10s place?

There are 100 three-digit numbers that have zero in the 10s place.

3.3 Adding and subtracting multiples of 10 and 100

> We are learning to add or subtract a multiple of 10 or 100 to or from a three-digit number.

Before we start

Write down the numbers that are missing from these number chains.

a) 587 →+10→ ? →+100→ ? →+10→ ? →+100→ ?

b) 951 →−100→ ? →−100→ ? →−10→ ? →−100→ ?

> We can use place value to help us add and subtract multiples of 10 or 100.

Let's learn

Nuria uses base 10 blocks to model 356 + 200.

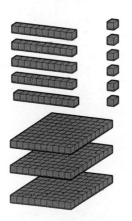 +

H	T	O
5	5	6

356 + 200 = 556   **556 = 5** hundreds + 5 tens + 6 ones

Amman uses base 10 blocks to model 621 − 400.

$621 − 400 = 221$

H	T	O
2	2	1

221 = **2** hundreds + 2 tens + 1 one

Let's practise

1) Work out how many hundreds are in each number then solve the problem. The first one has been done for you.

a) **3**00 + **4**00 = **3** hundreds add **4** hundreds = **7** hundreds = **7**00

b) 600 + 300 = **?**   c) 200 + 700 = **?**   d) 300 + 300 = **?**

e) 100 + 500 = **?**   f) 700 − 200 = **?**   g) 600 − 300 = **?**

h) 800 − 400 = **?**   i) 900 − 300 = **?**   j) 800 − 700 = **?**

2) Can you add and subtract these multiples of 100?

a) 683 + 200 = **?**

b) 500 + 243 = **?**

c) 920 − 300 = **?**

d) 469 − 100 = **?**

e) 551 + 400 = **?**

f) 600 + 102 = **?**

g) 523 − 400 = **?**

h) 609 − 500 = **?**

i) 470 + 500 = **?**

j) 940 − 600 = **?**

3) Finlay uses place value to calculate **645 + 50**.

Check your answers using base 10 blocks or place value counters.

He knows that 645 = 600 + 40 + 5
600 + 40 + **50** + 5 = 695

Use Finlay's method to calculate the answers to these additions and subtractions.

a) 253 + 40   b) 732 + 60   c) 343 + 30

d) 517 + 80   e) 694 – 30   f) 483 – 70

g) 295 – 50   h) 874 – 30   i) 962 – 20

4) Isla draws a number line to show that

345 – 70 = 275.

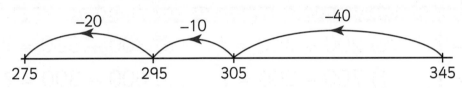

Write a number sentence for each number line.

a)

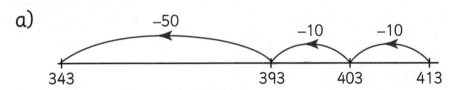

b)

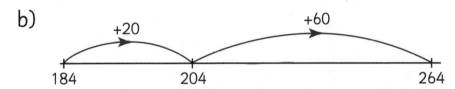

c)

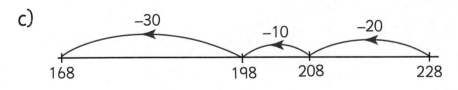

d)

-10 -10 -30

789   799   809   839

e)

$+20$ $+20$

576   596   616

5) Find the missing numbers.

a) $417 + \boxed{?} = 817$

b) $\boxed{?} + 673 = 713$

c) $\boxed{?} = 392 + 80$

d) $349 - \boxed{?} = 49$

e) $\boxed{?} - 60 = 210$

f) $\boxed{?} = 754 - 80$

⭐ CHALLENGE! ....

Copy and complete the number sentences.

Each missing number should be a multiple of 10 or 100. Compare your solutions with a partner. Is there more than one answer?

a) $530 - \boxed{?} - \boxed{?} = 400$

b) $530 - \boxed{?} - \boxed{?} - \boxed{?} = 380$

c) $650 - \boxed{?} - \boxed{?} - \boxed{?} = 400$

d) $650 - \boxed{?} - \boxed{?} - \boxed{?} - \boxed{?} = 390$

Number – addition and subtraction

3.4 Number bonds to 100

We are learning to find pairs of numbers that add up to 100.

Before we start

What number must go on the big owl to make each pair total 20?

a)

b)

c)

d)

e)

f)

Resource 1C_3.4_Before we start

Knowing the number bonds for 100 can help us to add and subtract efficiently.

Let's learn

Isla uses **partitioning** to check that **24 + 76 = 100**.

The 20 and the 70 make 90.
The 4 and the 6 make 10.
90 add 10 equals 100.

Nuria uses a 100-bead string to show that **100 − 24 = 76**.

10 20 30 40 50 60 70 76

−24

Finlay draws a number line to show that **100 − 76 = 24**.

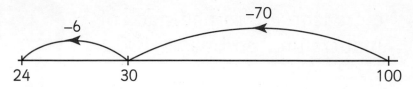

−6

−70

24   30   100

Amman draws a bar model to help him write a fact family for 100.

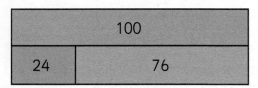

100	
24	76

24 + 76 = 100   100 − 24 = 76

76 + 24 = 100   100 − 76 = 24

Let's practise

1) Use a bead string or draw an empty number line to help you complete the number sentences.

a) 47 + [?] = 100   b) 53 + [?] = 100

c) 36 + [?] = 100   d) 21 + [?] = 100

e) 64 + [?] = 100   f) 18 + [?] = 100

g) 85 + [?] = 100   h) 92 + [?] = 100

i) 100 − 55 = [?]   j) 100 − 43 = [?]

k) 100 − 26 = [?]   l) 100 − 67 = [?]

2) Write a fact family for each bar model in your jotter.

a)
100	
73	27

b)
100	
35	65

c)
100	
84	16

d)
100	
48	52

3) Use partitioning to check whether each number sentence is true or false. Change one digit in each false number sentence to make it true.

a) 95 + 5 = 100   b) 37 + 73 = 100
c) 58 + 42 = 100   d) 29 + 81 = 100
e) 49 + 61 = 100   f) 87 + 17 = 100

★ CHALLENGE! ....

Number cards

Use these digit cards to make pairs of numbers that total 100.

A digit may only be used once in a calculation. For example:

3 **2** and **6** **8** makes 100

How many can you make? There are over 30 possibilities!

3.5 Doubling and halving

> We are learning to use doubling and halving to add and subtract two-digit numbers.

Before we start

Draw the number card that shows the answer to:

a) double 7 plus 1

b) double 6 minus 2

c) 1 less than double 9

d) 2 more than double 8

e) Which card is left over?
Write a 'double fact' for this number.

| 18 | 10 | 17 | 19 | 15 |

> Doubling and halving is a useful strategy for adding and subtracting two-digit numbers.

Let's learn

Finlay knows that **double 4 means 4 + 4 which equals 8**.

He uses this fact to work out that **double 40 is 40 + 40 = 80** and **double 400 is 400 + 400 = 800**.

Nuria knows that **half of 8 is 4**.

She uses this fact to work out that **half of 80 = 40** and **half of 800 = 400**.

Amman uses partitioning to work out **double 39**.

Double 30 = 60 and **double 9 = 18** so **double 39 is 60 plus 18 = 78**.

Isla uses partitioning to work out **half of 78**.

Half of 70 = 35 and **half of 8 = 4** so **half of 78 is 35 plus 4 = 39**.

Let's practise

1) Find the answers to these calculations using your knowledge of doubling and halving.

a) 60 + 60

b) 90 + 90

c) 300 + 300

d) 160 – 80

e) 140 – 70

f) 400 – 200

2) Double each number.

a) 49   b) 28   c) 57   d) 36

e) 84   f) 61   g) 95   h) 73

3) Halve each number.

a) 64   b) 48   c) 22   d) 88

e) 52   f) 76   g) 104   h) 212

CHALLENGE!

Isla made 240 by doubling two numbers.

a) What two numbers could she have used?

b) Write down addition number sentences to show how she might have done this.

3.6 Adding a string of numbers

> We are learning to add a string of numbers by looking for multiples of 10.

Before we start

Skittles and balls of the same colour should add up to make a multiple of 10.

a) Which pair is correct?

33 75 94 41 25 52   4 2 9 8 6 7

b) Change the number on the other balls so that each pair totals a multiple of 10.

c) Can you find another way by replacing the number on the ball with a two-digit number?

> Using multiples of 10 can help make tricky calculations easier.

Let's learn

Amman is adding 24 + 11 + 36.

First, he looks at the **ones** digits.

He knows that 4 + 6 = 10, so 24 + 36 will give a multiple of 10.

4 add 6 makes 10

20 add 30 makes 50

$$\overbrace{24 + 11 + 36}^{60} = 60 + 11 = 71$$

50 + 10 = 60 so 24 + 36 = **60**
60 + 11 = 71

70 + 40 = 110
Answer 114

When we have lots of numbers to add it is helpful to make jottings.

Amman adds **40 + 17 + 53 + 4**.
Talk about his jottings.

Let's practise

1) Look for a pair of numbers that total a multiple of 10 then add the third number.

a) 17 + 18 + 42   b) 37 + 23 + 40

c) 55 + 29 + 15   d) 21 + 26 + 24

e) 31 + 19 + 30   f) 44 + 16 + 21

2) Now try adding these number strings.

Make jottings to help you keep track of your thinking.

a) 13 7 21 16 9   b) 6 14 2 16 2

c) 5 45 8 19 31   d) 7 7 54 10 26

CHALLENGE!

Work with a partner. How many different ways can you find to make the number sentence true?
Each missing number must be a multiple of 5 or 10.

| ? | + | 20 | + | ? | = | 120 |

3.7 Adding and subtracting 8 or 9 using round and adjust

We are learning to add and subtract 8 or 9 to a number.

Before we start

Nuria has got muddled up. Explain what she has done wrong. Change each answer to make the number sentences correct.

a) 76 + 10 = 760
b) 39 + 10 = 390
c) 98 + 10 = 980
d) 62 – 10 = 62
e) 43 – 10 = 43
f) 105 – 10 = 105

We can use what we know about adding and subtracting 10 to add and subtract 8 or 9.

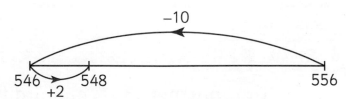

Let's learn

Nuria calculates **234 + 9** on a number line.

+10

234   243   244
            –1

Finlay calculates **556 – 8** on a number line.

–10

546   548   556
   +2

Talk about Nuria and Finlay's strategy. How could you use this strategy to calculate 234 + 8 and 556 – 9?

Number lines

1) For each of these questions, add or subtract 10 first.
Think about whether you have added or subtracted
one too many and then adjust your answer.
Use a number line to show your working.

For example: **37 + 9**   37 + 10 = 47 so 37 + 9 = 46

Now you try.

a) 58 + 9

58 + 10 = | ? | so 58 + 9 = | ? |

b) 43 – 9

43 – 10 = | ? | so 43 – 9 = | ? |

c) 79 + 9

79 + 10 = | ? | so 79 + 9 = | ? |

d) 61 – 9

61 – 10 = | ? | so 61 – 9 = | ? |

e) 55 + 9

55 + 10 = | ? | so 55 + 9 = | ? |

2) Amman has been given some addition and subtraction
calculations to do. He is using cubes to work out the answer
and it seems to be taking a while. Show Amman how he
can quickly work out each answer by changing the 8 into
10, then adjusting to find the answer.

a) 47 + 8   47 + 10 = | ? | so 47 + 8 = | ? |

b) 32 − 8   32 − 10 = ?   so 32 − 8 = ?

c) 68 + 8   68 + 10 = ?   so 68 + 8 = ?

d) 83 − 8   83 − 10 = ?   so 83 − 8 = ?

e) 72 + 8   72 + 10 = ?   so 72 + 8 = ?

f) 55 − 8   55 − 10 = ?   so 55 − 8 = ?

g) 75 + 8   75 + 10 = ?   so 75 + 8 = ?

h) 36 − 8   36 − 10 = ?   so 36 − 8 = ?

3) Copy and complete each number sentence in your jotter.
   Explain to a partner how you worked each answer out.

   a) 87 + ? = 96   b) ? + 53 = 61   c) 74 + ? = 82

   d) ? + 33 = 42   e) 91 − ? = 82   f) 85 − ? = 76

   g) 46 − ? = 38   h) ? − 9 = 71   i) ? − 8 = 66

⭐ CHALLENGE! ....

Write down all the different three-digit
numbers you can make using these
digit cards.

2   4   7   1

a) Add 8 or 9 to each number you have made.

b) Subtract 8 or 9 from each number you have made.

3.8 Solving number problems

We are learning to choose a strategy to solve a number problem.

Before we start

Complete the number puzzles. Numbers in each row and column must add up to the total in the grey boxes.

a)

9		16
		13
15		

b)

		17
	5	
19	16	

When solving number problems it is important to choose a strategy you feel confident with.

Let's learn

There are many strategies that we can use to solve number problems.

Use known facts

For example: 7 − 3 = 4 so 57 − 3 = 54
18 + 2 = 20 so 180 + 20 = 200

Doubling and halving

For example: double 21 is 42 so 21 + 21 = 42
half of 86 is 43 so 86 − 43 = 43

Partitioning

For example: $37 + 45 \rightarrow 30 + 40 = 70$ and $7 + 5 = 12$
$70 + 12 = 82$

$69 - 15 \rightarrow 60 - 10 = 50$ and $9 - 5 = 4$
$50 + 4 = 54$

Look for multiples of 10 or 100

For example:

$52 + 67 + 48 \rightarrow 52 + 48 = 100 \rightarrow 100 + 67 = 167$

Add or subtract 10 then adjust

For example: $124 + 9 = 124 + 10 - 1 = 133$
$257 - 8 = 257 - 10 + 2 = 249$

Count on or count back

For example: $396 + \boxed{?} = 403$

Think 'part-part-whole'

For example: $\boxed{?} - 76 = 24$

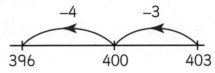

1) Find the answer to each subtraction using a strategy of your choice. Use the same numbers to write an addition partner for each subtraction. The first one has been done for you.

a)

b) $66 - 33 = ?$ $? + ? = ?$

c) $72 - 9 = ?$ $? + ? = ?$

d) $47 - 12 = ?$ $? + ? = ?$

e) $33 - 16 = ?$ $? + ? = ?$

f) $84 - 23 = ?$ $? + ? = ?$

2) Solve these number problems. Write your answers in your jotter. Explain to a partner how you worked each answer out.

a) $767 + ? = 775$ b) $? + 120 = 240$

c) $109 + 8 = ?$ d) $350 - ? = 270$

e) $810 - ? = 405$ f) $? - 7 = 500$

g) $486 - ? = 406$ h) $? - 900 = 12$

i) $122 = 131 - ?$ j) $6 + 32 + 6 + 18 = ?$

k) $300 + 400 + 13 + 13 = ?$

⭐ CHALLENGE! ....

What is the number?

a) I am thinking of a number. I subtract 23, then add 48 and my answer is 205. What number am I thinking of?

b) Think of a number between 100 and 1000 and write your own 'What is my number?' challenge.

Swap your challenge with a partner. Solve each other's challenges.

3.9 Solving word problems

> We are learning to solve addition and subtraction word problems.

Before we start

There are 15 balls and 29 bats.
How many bats won't have a ball?

> I think this is an addition problem.

> I think it's a subtraction problem.

Who do you agree with? Explain your thinking.

> The same word problem can be solved in different ways. It is important to choose the way you feel most confident with.

Let's learn

Isla and Nuria are solving this word problem.

There are 100 children in the school. 54 are boys. How many girls are there?

Isla thinks, '54 and what makes 100?'

$54 + \boxed{?} = 100$

Isla draws an empty number line.

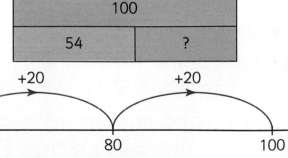

100	
54	?

Then she counts on from 54 up to 100. $6 + 40 = 46$.

Nuria thinks, '100 take away 54 makes what?'

$100 - 54 = \boxed{?}$

She partitions 54 into 50 + 4.

$$100 - 50 = 50$$
$$50 - 4 = 46$$

Jottings help her to keep track of her thinking.

Let's practise

Solve these word problems using a strategy of your choice.

1) 263 adults arrive to see the school concert. Eight adults don't get a seat. How many seats are there?

2) There is double the number of blue pencils than red pencils in a box. If there are 49 red pencils, how many blue pencils are there?

3) There are 175 fans in the north stand and 11 fewer fans in the south stand. How many fans are in the south stand?

4) Finlay's grandpa has some chickens and 158 sheep. There are 188 animals altogether. How many chickens are there?

CHALLENGE!

Write a word problem that can be solved by adding or subtracting. Your problem must have at least one three-digit number in it. Challenge a partner to solve your problem. Ask your partner for a problem for you to solve.

3.10 Adding two- and three-digit numbers

> We are learning to add a two-digit number to a three-digit number.

Before we start

Use the numbers and symbols on the cards to make as many additions and subtractions as you can. Use five cards each time. Cards may be used once only in each calculation.

| 17 | + | 14 | 3 | 8 | – | 11 | = |

> Partitioning numbers according to their place values can help us with addition.

Let's learn

Amman and Nuria are adding 83 + 675.

They keep the larger number whole and **partition** the smaller number: **675 + 83 = 675 + 80 + 3**

They each draw an empty number line.

Amman's number line:

+30   +50   +3

675   705   755 758

Nuria's number line:

+80   +3

675   755 758

How would **you** use a number line to solve this problem?

1) Draw an empty number line for each addition then solve it. Compare number lines and answers with a partner.
   a) 515 + 87   b) 246 + 76   c) 58 + 632
   d) 42 + 488   e) 374 + 69   f) 35 + 797

2) The children think about different ways to solve these additions. Talk about their strategies.

812 + 26   **73 + 127**   **934 + 19**

812 = **800 + 10 + 2**
26 = **20 + 6**
800 + 10 + 20 = 830
830 + **2 + 6** = 838

73 + 27 = 100
so
73 + 127 = 200

934 + 20 = 954
so
934 + 19 = 953

3) Think about how to solve these additions. Choose the strategy you feel most confident with.
   a) 231 + 28   b) 55 + 345   c) 810 + 39
   d) 119 + 51   e) 715 + 46   f) 312 + 58
   g) 426 + 29   h) 94 + 101   i) 506 + 74

CHALLENGE!

Create your own questions with these answers. Put a two-digit number in one box and a three-digit number in the other box. Challenge a partner to turn your additions into subtractions. Turn your partner's additions into subtractions.

a) [?] + [?] = 306   b) [?] + [?] = 640

3.11 Subtracting two-digit numbers from three-digit numbers

We are learning to subtract a two-digit number from a three-digit number.

Before we start

Write the missing numbers in your jotter.

a)
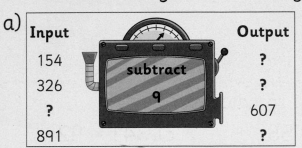

Input	Output
154	?
326	?
?	607
891	?

subtract 9

b)
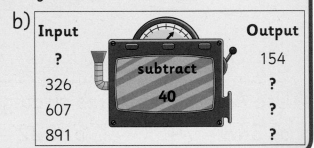

Input	Output
?	154
326	?
607	?
891	?

subtract 40

Partitioning and place value can help us with subtraction.

Let's learn

Amman and Isla are calculating **753 – 77**

They each draw an empty number line to help them solve the problem.

Amman's number line:

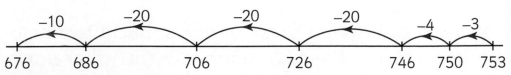

−4   −20   −3   −50
676   680   700   703   753

Isla's number line:

−10   −20   −20   −20   −4   −3
676   686   706   726   746   750   753

753 – 77 = 676

Finlay and Nuria are calculating **959 – 34**

959 = 900 and **50** and **9**   **34 = 30** and **4**

900 and (**50 – 30**) and (**9 – 4**) = **900** and **20** and **5** = **925**

They use place value counters to check their answer.

Talk about the children's strategies.

Would Amman and Isla's strategy work for 959 – 34?

Would Finlay and Nuria's strategy work for 753 – 77?

Let's practise

1) Use Amman and Isla's strategy to calculate:

    a) 548 – 79   b) 822 – 56   c) 341 – 92

    d) 707 – 28   e) 440 – 67   f) 214 – 85

    g) 600 – 31   h) 933 – 48   i) 725 – 95

2) Use Finlay and Nuria's strategy to calculate:

    a) 965 – 42   b) 499 – 75   c) 858 – 36

    d) 384 – 62   e) 774 – 51   f) 131 – 11

    g) 298 – 55   h) 693 – 43   i) 577 – 44

CHALLENGE!

Now try these. Think carefully about your choice of strategy. Use a number line, place value counters or base 10 blocks to help you.

a) 200 – **?** = 43   b) 656 – **?** = 224

c) 901 – **?** = 820   d) **?** – 59 = 111

e) **?** – 44 = 700   f) **?** – 516 = 75

3.12 Adding three-digit numbers

We are learning to add three-digit numbers together.

Before we start

Isla is unsure which strategy to use. Explain how you would solve each addition, then find the answers.

Can you please help?

a) 255 + 45   b) 19 + 106   c) 35 + 914   d) 546 + 28

The same addition problem can be presented and solved in different ways.

Let's learn

Additions can be written vertically or horizontally. For example:

286 + 363 means the same as

```
  286
+ 363
_____
```

Nuria keeps 363 whole and partitions 286 into 200 + 40 + 40 + 6.

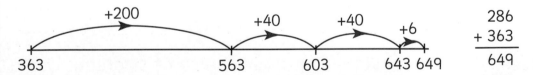

```
  286
+ 363
_____
  649
```

Amman partitions both numbers into hundreds, tens and ones. He adds the hundreds first, then the tens, then the ones.

Lastly he adds the totals together.

```
  200  and  80  and  6
+ 300  and  60  and  3
─────────────────────
  500  and 140  and  9   = 600 + 40 + 9
```

H	T	O
2	8	6
3	6	3

6	4	9

Nuria and Amman lay out base 10 blocks and count in hundreds, tens and ones to check their answer.

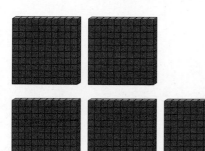  

100, 200, 300, 400, 500   510, 520, 530....................640   641...............649

Let's practise

1) Draw a number line to calculate the answers to these additions.

  a)   573   b)   278   c)   487
      + 259   + 643   + 366

  d)   428   e)   386   f)   578
      + 347   + 145   + 418

  g) 547 + 278   h) 675 + 248   i) 360 + 569

2) Solve these additions by partitioning both numbers.

  a)   145   b)   259   c)   515
      + 783   + 335   + 237

d)　252
　　+ 458

e)　374
　　+ 364

f)　148
　　+ 627

g) 802 + 157　　h) 416 + 477　　i) 263 + 144

3) Finlay adds 246 + 199 mentally.

Use Finlay's strategy to find the sum of these number pairs.

a) 602 and 99
b) 199 and 518
c) 455 and 399
d) 64 and 799
e) 283 and 299
f) 499 and 170
g) 399 and 580
h) 101 + 699
i) 399 + 499

I know that 199 is one less than 200.

246 + 200 = 446.

I have added one too many.

I need to adjust my answer by taking one away.

446 take away one makes 445 so 246 + 199 = 445.

4) Complete the number statements below.

a) 270 + ? = 815

b) 165 + ? = 513

c) ? + 287 = 343

d) 469 + ? = 523

5) Now try adding these numbers.

a) 374 + 326 + 100
c) 199 + 160 + 340

b) 140 + 140 + 712
d) 201 + 399 + 56

CHALLENGE!

Isla is thinking of two three-digit numbers that total 800.
The numbers have a difference of 302.
What two numbers is Isla thinking of?

? ? ? + ? ? ? = 8 0 0

3.13 Subtracting three-digit numbers

We are learning to subtract a three-digit number from another three-digit number.

Before we start

Use these numbers to make six different subtractions and solve them. Choose a number from the yellow box and a number from the orange box each time. Think carefully about your choice of strategy.

612	735
260	
409	500
388	

18	32
99	
76	53
67	

The same subtraction problem can be presented and solved in different ways.

Let's learn

Subtractions can be written vertically or horizontally.
For example:

854 – 621 means the same as

$$854$$
$$- 621$$

Isla keeps 854 whole and partitions 621 into 600 and 20 and 1.

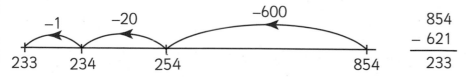

```
         −1    −20        −600
233    234    254              854
```

$$854$$
$$- 621$$
$$233$$

Finlay partitions both numbers into hundreds, tens and ones. He subtracts the hundreds first, then the tens, then the ones.

```
   800 and 50 and 4
 − 600 and 20 and 1
   200 and 30 and 3   = 233
```

H	T	O
8	5	4
6	2	1
2	3	3

Isla and Finlay check their answer by laying out place value counters and removing some of them.

$800 - 600 = \textbf{200}$ and $50 - 20 = \textbf{30}$ and $4 - 1 = \textbf{3}$

Let's practise

1) Use an empty number line to calculate the answers to these subtractions.

  a)   503
      − 197

  b)   426
      − 274

  c)   900
      − 516

  d)   718
      − 350

  e)   603
      − 416

  f)   231
      − 194

  g) 400 − 389   h) 811 − 661   i) 705 − 507

2) Solve these subtractions by partitioning both numbers.

  a)   875
      − 321

  b)   536
      − 112

  c)   789
      − 563

  d)   648
      − 407

  e)   978
      − 827

  f)   456
      − 213

  g) 599 − 123   h) 686 − 254   i) 791 − 740

3) Decide if each number sentence is true or false.
Change the false statements to make them true.
a) 267 − 99 = 168
b) 400 − 199 = 201
c) 150 − 99 = 151
d) 745 − 299 = 444
e) 600 − 599 = 100
f) 650 − 399 = 249

4) Two numbers have a difference of 283.
If the smaller number is 563, what is the larger number?

CHALLENGE!

Work with a partner.

- Choose any three digits from the cards below to make a three-digit number. The largest digit must be first.

- Now write your number backwards.

- Subtract the smaller number from the larger number to give a new number.

- Take your new three-digit number and write it backwards.

- Add these two numbers together and write down the answer.

- Do the same thing again with a different set of digits. What do you notice? Does this always work?

For example
924
429
924 − 429 = 495
495 + 594 = 1089

3.14 Representing and solving word problems

> We are learning to represent the same word problem in different ways.

Before we start

What number is each girl thinking about?
Explain how you worked each answer out.

> My number is the sum of 417 and 248.

> My number is the difference between 512 and 176.

> Representing the same problem in different ways helps us to understand it better.

Let's learn

Amman and Finlay use a Think Board to help them solve a word problem.

First, they draw a bar model. Then, they use an empty number line to find the answer.

They write a number sentence to show how they worked it out. Finally, they write their answer in the centre.

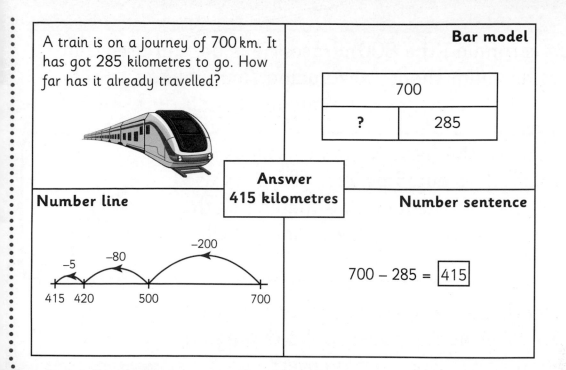

A train is on a journey of 700 km. It has got 285 kilometres to go. How far has it already travelled?

Bar model

700	
?	285

**Answer
415 kilometres**

Number line

```
        -200
   -80  ⌒
 -5 ⌒  ⌒
⌒
415 420   500      700
```

Number sentence

700 − 285 = 415

Let's practise

Draw a Think Board for each question, then solve the problem.

Think board

1) Finlay and Nuria are seeing who can bounce a ball the most times. Finlay manages 148 bounces. Nuria manages 196 bounces. How many more bounces did Nuria manage?

2) 462 children are at a concert. There are 379 more adults than children. How many adults are at the concert?

3) At the end of a football match there are 582 people still watching. At the start of the match there were 748. How many people went home during the match?

4) Amman is running the 800 m race. He is getting tired, but he hears his mum shout, 'Keep going Amman! You've only got 145 m left.' How far has Amman already run?

5) At the start of the year, Nuria's class was given a box of coloured pencils. The class used up or lost 247 of them and by the end of the year there were 163 left. How many pencils were in the box to begin with?

6) Mrs Green buys 156 new books for the school library. She wants to cover all the books, but she only has 137 covers. How many books won't get a cover?

7) Auntie Sue has delivered 243 letters. When she stops for lunch she still has 178 to deliver. How many letters did she start with?

★ CHALLENGE!

Write your own word problem with at least one three-digit number in it. Challenge your friends to create a Think Board for your problem and solve it.

3.15 Two-step word problems

We are learning to solve two-step word problems.

Before we start

Solve this word problem using a strategy of your choice. Explain how you solved it.

A farmer had 245 sheep. He sold some at the market. Now he has 182. How many sheep did the farmer sell?

Sometimes we need to perform more than one calculation to solve a word problem.

Let's learn

I'm saving up to buy a new bike costing £429. I've already saved £217 and I got £126 for my birthday. Do I have enough? If not, how much more will I need to save?

This word problem has two steps. We need to do two separate calculations to solve it.

Step 1: Find out how much money Amman has got so far.

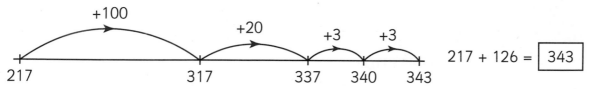

$$217 + 126 = \boxed{343}$$

Amman has **£343** so far.

Step 2: Ask yourself, 'Does he have enough?' If not, work out how much more he needs.

Amman needs £429. He does not have enough.

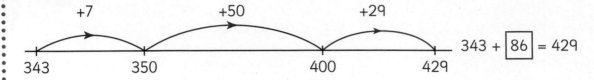

$343 + \boxed{86} = 429$

Amman needs another **£86**.

Let's practise

Solve these two-step word problems.
Choose the strategies you feel most confident with.

1) P4 are raising money for charity. Their sponsored spell raises £346 and their cake and candy sale raises £138. How much more money do they still need to reach their target of £650?

2) Isla wants to make 950 ml of fruit punch for her party. She needs 450 ml of orange juice, 205 ml of pineapple juice, 80 ml of strawberry cordial and some lemonade. How much lemonade does Isla need?

3) On Saturday 320 people visited the sports centre. On Sunday there were 208 more visitors than on Saturday. How many people visited the sports centre over the weekend?

4) Amman, Finlay and Nuria are playing a computer game. Amman scores 239 points, Finlay scores 289 points and Nuria scores 26 points less than Finlay. How many points did the children score altogether?

5) Finlay is 122 cm tall. Isla is 5 cm taller than Nuria and Nuria is 13 cm shorter than Finlay. How tall are Isla and Nuria?

6) In one week a shop sells some apples, 112 pears and 261 tomatoes. If 515 pieces of fruit were sold altogether, how many apples did the shop sell?

⭐ CHALLENGE!

Write your own two-step word problems to fit this bar model. Each problem should have one of the numbers in the bar model as the answer.

135		
21	35	79

Try to make four problems, each one with a different answer.

4.1 Dividing by skip counting

> We are learning to use repeated addition or subtraction to solve division problems.

Before we start

Isla saves her pocket money. If she gets £5 every week, how much does she have saved after six weeks?

> We can use skip counting to help us solve division problems.

Let's learn

Nuria and Finlay are working out the answer to 20 ÷ 5.

Nuria skip counts backwards in fives from 20 to 0 to work out her answer:

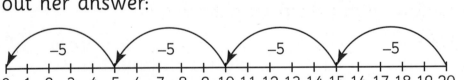

There are four jumps backwards from 20 to 0, so she works out 20 ÷ 5 = 4.

Finlay skip counts forward to work out his answer:

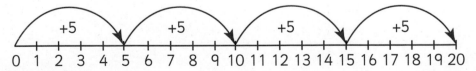

There are four jumps forward from 0 to 20, so he gets the same answer.
20 ÷ 5 = 4

Let's practise

1) Skip count to work out how many people are in **each** minibus and write a division sentence in your jotter to show your answer.

a) There are 12 people in two minibuses.

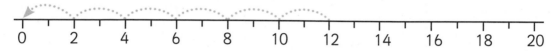

b) There are 15 people in five minibuses.

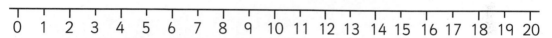

c) There are 25 people in five minibuses.

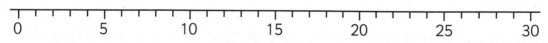

2) Amman has 21 sweets and shares them between himself, Nuria and Isla. How many do they each get?

Use skip counting to work out this problem and write a division sentence to show your answer.

You could use a number line to help you.

CHALLENGE!

Help the cinema owner to solve a tricky problem:

Standard tickets for the cinema cost £7 each. Today the cinema made a total of £280 from selling standard tickets. How many standard tickets did the cinema sell?

4.2 Dividing with remainders

We are learning that some division problems have remainders.

Before we start

Amman's class has 25 children. His teacher puts them into groups of five. How many groups are there?

When we work out division problems, sometimes there are leftovers. We call these **remainders**.

Let's learn

Nuria has baked nine cupcakes and wants to share them with Isla.

Nuria   Isla

When they share them out, they both get four each but one is left over. That one is the **remainder.**

We can record the problem like this:

$9 \div 2 = 4$, remainder 1

We shorten this to:

$9 \div 2 = 4 \text{ r } 1$

Let's practise

1) Finlay is sharing out fruit. For each problem, say if there will be any leftovers and how many.

   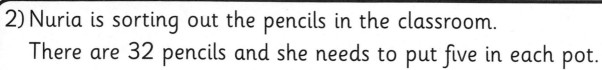

   a) Seven apples shared between three children.
   b) 12 oranges shared between five children.
   c) 30 grapes shared between five children.
   d) 11 cherries shared between two children.

2) Nuria is sorting out the pencils in the classroom.

   There are 32 pencils and she needs to put five in each pot.

   a) How many pots will she need?
   b) How many pencils will be leftover?

3) Work out these problems and record any remainders. The first one has been done for you.

   a) 16 ÷ 3 = 5 r 1   b) 21 ÷ 5   c) 64 ÷ 10
   d) 17 ÷ 2   e) 24 ÷ 3   f) 33 ÷ 5

CHALLENGE!

Amman has 60 bulbs to plant in the garden. He is trying to decide how many to plant in each row so that all the rows are equal with none left over. Can you help him work out all the ways he could plant the rows so that no bulbs would be left over?

4.3 Solving multiplication problems

We are learning to use facts we know to solve multiplication problems.

Before we start

Nuria thinks of a number. She doubles it and gets 18. What was the number she was thinking of?

When we are working out multiplication problems, we can use facts that we know to help us.

Let's learn

Amman, Isla and Finlay are working out 4 × 5.

Amman skip counts in 5s to work out the answer: 5 ... 10 ... 15 ... **20**

Isla thinks she has a different way to solve the problem.

She knows that double 5 is 10, so she adds 10 and 10 to get her answer of **20**.

Finlay has another way. He already knows that 3 × 5 = 15, so he just adds another 5 to 15 to get his answer of **20**.

We can use facts we know to work out multiplication problems in different ways.

1) Make or draw an array for each of these questions and think about how you could use your knowledge of doubles to help you work out these problems. Explain how you work out your answers.

a) 5 × 8   b) 6 × 5   c) 4 × 4   d) 6 × 3

2) Think about ways you could solve these problems using facts you know and explain how you work out your answer.

a) Class 3 are planting flowers in a garden. There are four rows each with space for nine flowers. How many flowers can be planted altogether?

b) There are 10 classes in school. Each class submits three poems for the school magazine. How many poems is that in total?

c) Isla has completed seven levels of a computer game and scored five bonus points on each level. How many bonus points does she have?

3) a) Write a multiplication sentence for this array and work out the answer.

b) Can you use this answer to work out the answer to 5 × 3?

c) What about 3 × 3?

CHALLENGE!

Can you invent your own word problems for each of these challenges?

a) Write a word problem that can be answered by doubling.

b) Write a division word problem with the answer 8.

c) Write a word problem where you could use a multiplication fact you already know to help.

4.4 Multiplying by 100

We are learning to multiply by 100.

Before we start

a) What is the value of the 8 in this number?
b) What is the value of the 4 in this number?

482

We can use different materials to explore what happens when we multiply numbers by 10.

Let's learn

We could use place value materials to see what happens when we multiply 3 by 100.

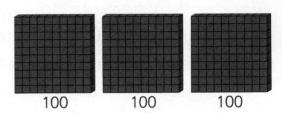

100   100   100

$3 \times 100 = 300$

When we multiply by 100, the number gets 100 times bigger.

	HUNDREDS	TENS	ONES
3×100	3	0	0

We can see that the ones digit has moved two places to the hundreds column and in the spaces for the tens and ones we put zeros as placeholders.

1) Use place value materials to work out these problems:

   a) 4×100 b) 5×100 c) 9×100 d) 8×100

2) Work out what number goes under the paint splashes for these problems:

   a) $100 \times$ ※ $= 600$ b) ※ $\times 100 = 200$

   c) ※ $\times 100 = 700$ d) $100 \times$ ※ $= 300$

3) Amman works out that ten £10 notes would be worth £100. How much would ten £100 notes be worth?

★ **CHALLENGE!** ....

Work with a partner. You will need a set of numeral cards from 1 to 10. Turn the cards over and shuffle them. Take it in turns to pick a card and multiply it by 100. Check if they are right!

Try multiplying your numeral cards by 1000.

Number cards

| 1 | 2 | 3 | 4 | 5 | 6 | 7 | 8 | 9 | 10 |

4.5 Dividing by 100

> We are learning to divide by 100.

Before we start

You have three £100 notes, nine £10 notes and five £1 coins. How much do you have altogether?

> When we divide by 100, the number gets 100 times smaller.

Let's learn

If we had a bar of chocolate with 100 squares and shared it between 100 people, they would all get one square each.

When we divide by 100, the number gets 100 times smaller.

100 ÷ 100

HUNDREDS	TENS	ONES
1	0	0
		1

We can see that the digits move two places to the right, from the hundreds to the ones column.

1) Use place value materials to work out these problems by grouping them into hundreds:
   a) 200 ÷ 100   b) 700 ÷ 100
   c) 400 ÷ 100   d) 900 ÷ 100

2) Work out what number goes under the paint splashes for these problems:
   a) ✱ ÷ 100 = 6   b) ✱ ÷ 100 = 3
   c) ✱ ÷ 100 = 8   d) ✱ ÷ 100 = 5

3) How many £100 notes would you need to make £1000? Write a division sentence to show your answer.

CHALLENGE!

Isla thinks of a number. She multiplies it by 100 and then doubles it to get 800. What number did she start with?

Make up more problems like this for a partner.

4.6 Linking multiplication and division

We are learning the relationship between multiplication and division.

Before we start

Can you show two different ways to work out the answer to 6 × 5?

We can use arrays to help us see the relationship between multiplication and division.

Let's learn

Amman is working out 15 ÷ 5. He gets 15 counters and sorts them into groups of five:

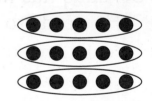

There are three groups of five so 15 ÷ 5 = 3.

Amman spots something else. When he looks at the counters, he can see that the array he has made also shows 3 × 5 = 15.

Multiplication is the opposite action of division. We call this the **inverse relationship** between multiplication and division.

If we know that 15 ÷ 5 = 3, then we also know 3 × 5 = 15. We can reverse division sentences and write them as multiplication sentences.

1) Can you reverse these division sentences to turn them into multiplication sentences? The first one has been done for you.
   a) 20 ÷ 5 = 4 reversed is 4 × 5 = 20
   b) 60 ÷ 10 = 6
   c) 14 ÷ 2 = 7
   d) 45 ÷ 5 = 9

You could make an array to help you.

2) Write a multiplication sentence and a division sentence for each array. The first array has been done for you.

   a) 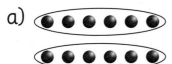   2 × 6 = 12   b) ● ● ● ● ●
                                    12 ÷ 2 = 6   ● ● ● ● ●
                                                           ● ● ● ● ●
                                                           ● ● ● ● ●
                                                           ● ● ● ● ●

   c) ● ● ● ● ● ● ● ● ● ●   d) ● ● ●
      ● ● ● ● ● ● ● ● ● ●   ● ● ●
      ● ● ● ● ● ● ● ● ● ●   ● ● ●
                                     ● ● ●

3) Finlay has made 40 muffins for the school fair.
   He needs to put 10 on each tray.
   a) Use multiplication to work out how many trays he will need.
   b) Write a multiplication sentence and a division sentence to show the answer to this problem.

CHALLENGE!

Nuria has written two division and multiplication number sentences. They both contain the same numbers.
The red rectangle is covering up a three-digit number.
What could the two numbers be?

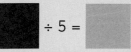 ÷ 5 = 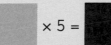   × 5 =

How do you know that the blue square is not covering up a one-digit number?

4.7 Recalling multiplication and division facts for 2, 5 and 10

We are learning to recall multiplication facts for 2, 5 and 10.

Before we start

Isla has 16 pencils in her pencil case. Nuria has half that number. How many pencils does Nuria have?

Recalling multiplication facts means knowing them straight away without having to work them out.

Let's learn

It is very useful to know multiplication and division facts as instant recall because we can use this knowledge to help us solve multiplication and division problems.

We can also link other knowledge we already have.

If we know doubles and halves up to 20, then we already know multiplication and division facts for 2.

Isla knows that double 4 is 8 so she also knows $4 \times 2 = 8$.

Finlay knows that half of 6 is 3 so he also knows $6 \div 2 = 3$.

If we know how many tens are in decade numbers, then we already know multiplication and division facts for 10.

Amman knows that there are three tens in 30, so he also knows that $3 \times 10 = 30$ and $30 \div 10 = 3$.

Let's practise

1) Use your knowledge of multiplication facts for 2, 5 and 10 to answer these questions.

   a) 5 × 2 =

   b) 9 multiplied by 2 is

   c) 3 lots of 2 are

   d) 2 × 2 =

   e) 7 × 2 =

   f) 8 groups of 2 are

2) Use your knowledge of multiplication facts to find the missing number.

3) Use your knowledge of multiplication and division facts to complete these triangles. Write two facts for each.

  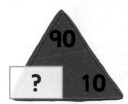

⭐ **CHALLENGE!** ....

Make some number triangles of your own. Each one must contain the number 6, 7 or 8.

Cover up one of the numbers using your thumb. Ask a friend to work out the answer by using multiplication or division facts.

Ask them to give you some triangle challenges too!

4.8 Multiplying and dividing using known facts

> We are learning to use facts we know to solve problems involving two- and three-digit numbers.

Before we start

Nuria runs 2 km each day. How many days does it take her to run a total of 20 km?

> We can use our knowledge of multiplication and division facts and then multiply or divide by 10 or 100 to help us work out problems involving bigger numbers.

Let's learn

We have learned in previous units that when we multiply by 10 the digits move one place to the left and when we multiply by 100 the digits move two places to the left.

We use zero as a placeholder:

For example, 9 × 10 = 90 and 9 × 100 = 900.

When we divide by 10 the digits move one place to the right and when we divide by 100 the digits move two places to the right:

For example, 90 ÷ 10 = 9 and 900 ÷ 100 = 9.

We can use this knowledge and other facts we know to help us work out problems.

Finlay is working out 2 × 400.

He knows that 2 × 200 = 400. He doubles this to get his answer: 2 × 400 = 800.

Amman is working out 5 × 30. He already knows that 5 × 3 = 15, then he multiplies this by 10 to get his answer: 5 × 30 = 150.

Let's practise

1) Use your knowledge of multiplying by 10 or 100 to help you work out these problems.

   a) 20 × 10   b) 3 × 20   c) 5 × 200   d) 400 × 2

2) Use your knowledge of dividing by 10 and 100 to help you work out these problems.

   Isla has done the first one for you.
   a) 400 ÷ 2 = 200
   b) 90 ÷ 3
   c) 500 ÷ 10
   d) 800 ÷ 2

   I know that 400 is 4 hundreds. I also know 4 ÷ 2 is 2. 4 hundreds divided by 2 is 2 hundreds, which is 200.

3) The children are going on a trip. The minibus can take 20 children at a time. How many minibuses will they need for these numbers of children:

   a) 200 children   b) 60 children
   c) 100 children   d) 140 children

CHALLENGE!

Finlay thinks of a number. He multiplies it by 3, then divides it by 100 and gets the answer 9. What number was he thinking of?

Isla thinks of a number. She divides it by 5, then multiplies it by 100 and gets the answer 1000. What number was she thinking of?

Make up more problems like this for a partner.

4.9 Solving number problems

We are learning to solve problems using a combination of addition, subtraction, multiplication and division.

Before we start

Finlay is skip counting to work out the answer to 9×5 and gets the answer 35. Think of another strategy he could use to solve this problem and work out if his answer is correct.

Some problems involve a combination of addition, subtraction, multiplication or division.

Let's learn

When solving a problem, we first need to decide which operation to use – addition, subtraction, multiplication or division. Sometimes, solving problems involves two of these operations.

Isla and Nuria go shopping. Isla buys two books that cost £10 each and Nuria buys five books that cost £5 each.

How much did they spend altogether?

First, use **multiplication** to work out how much they both spent.

$2 \times 10 = 20$, so Isla spent £20. $5 \times 5 = 25$, so Nuria spent £25.

Then use **addition** to work out the total that they spent.

$20 + 25 = 45$, so they spent £45 altogether.

Let's practise

1) Amman and Finlay both collect stickers.
Each packet contains five stickers.
Amman buys six packets of stickers.
Finlay buys four packets of stickers.

Show how you work out each part of the problem.

a) How many stickers does Amman have?
b) How many stickers does Finlay have?
c) How many more does Amman have?

2) Nuria's family is going to the funfair. It costs £5 per adult and £3 per child. How much would it cost altogether for:

a) 2 adults and 3 children   b) 4 adults and 2 children
c) 3 adults and 5 children   d) 5 adults and 10 children

Show how you work out each part of the problem.

3) Isla and Finlay are helping organise the sports hall for games. Isla gets 20 hoops from the cupboard and carries five each time. Finlay gets 10 balls from the cupboard and carries two each time. Work out how many trips to the cupboard they take altogether. Record how you work out the problem.

CHALLENGE!

Word problem

Finlay has £16 in the bank. He gets a job and earns £5 each week.
How much does he have altogether when he has worked for nine weeks?

Think board

a) Use a Think Board to represent the problem in different ways and work out the answer.

b) Make up your own Think Board for a partner to work out.

5.1 Finding part of a set

We are learning to find part of a set.

Before we start

Nuria has a bag containing 20 sweets. One quarter of them are strawberry-flavoured. How many strawberry-flavoured sweets does she have?

We can use a bar model to help us find any fraction of an amount.

Let's learn

Finlay has a bag containing **12 sweets**:

We can solve this using a bar model:

I am going to eat **three-quarters** of my sweets. How many sweets will I eat?

quarters tells us to split the bar into four equal parts:

whole bag

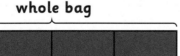

12 tells us the number of sweets to be shared out:

whole bag

three tells us how many parts Finlay eats:

Three-quarters of **12** sweets = **9** sweets

Finlay eats **nine sweets**.

whole bag

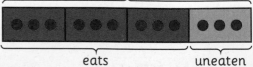

eats   uneaten

1) Find the following:

   a) Three-quarters of 16 apples:

   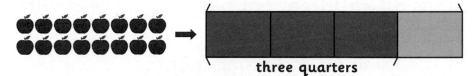

   three quarters

   b) Two-thirds of nine pens:

   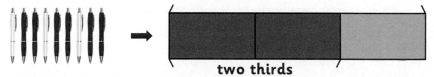

   two thirds

   c) Two-fifths of 20 pencils:

   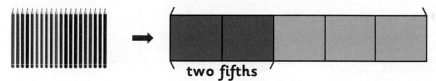

   two fifths

   d) Five-sixths of 12 toy soldiers:

   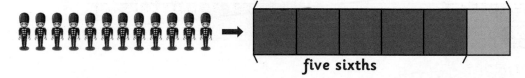

   five sixths

2) Draw bar models to solve the following:

   a) Two-**thirds** of 18 children = ___?___ children.

   b) Five-**sixths** of £24 = ___?___.

   c) Three-**eighths** of 40 stickers = ___?___ stickers.

   d) Four-**fifths** of 35 jotters = ___?___ jotters.

   Resource
   1C_5.1_Let's_
   practise_Q2

3) Draw bar models to solve the following:

a) Isla had **£21**. She spent **two-thirds** of it on new headphones. How much were the headphones?

b) A class has **30 children**. **Four-sixths** of the children are girls. How many girls are there?

c) Amman is cycling **40 miles** for charity. He's cycled **three-quarters** so far. How far has he cycled?

CHALLENGE!

Find the missing numbers:

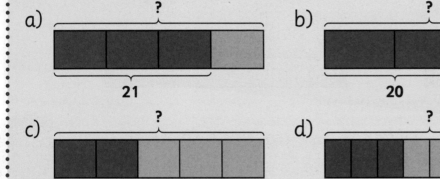

a)
?
21

b)
?
20

c)
?
12

d)
?
9

Make up three similar problems for your partner to solve.

5.2 Making a whole

We are learning to make a whole.

Before we start

Say the name of each fraction and match the equivalent fractions.

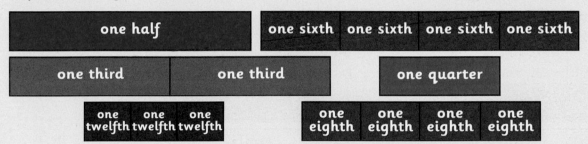

We can use fractions to make one whole in different ways.

Let's learn

Isla takes one half from the pile of fraction cards:

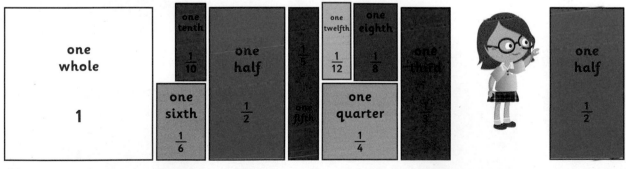

She has been asked to make one whole by choosing from the pile:

I could take another half to make one whole.

one half $\frac{1}{2}$ | one half $\frac{1}{2}$ is the same as one whole 1

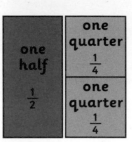
You could also have chosen two quarters to make one whole.

one half $\frac{1}{2}$ | one quarter $\frac{1}{4}$ / one quarter $\frac{1}{4}$ is the same as one whole 1

Can you find any other ways that Isla can make one whole?

Let's practise

1) How much more do the children need to make one whole?

a) Isla has **one quarter**:

one quarter $\frac{1}{4}$

b) Nuria has **one third**:

c) Amman has **three fifths**:

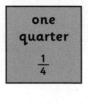

$\frac{1}{5}$ $\frac{1}{5}$ $\frac{1}{5}$

one fifth | one fifth | one fifth

d) Finlay has **five eighths**:

one eighth $\frac{1}{8}$ | one eighth $\frac{1}{8}$ | one eighth $\frac{1}{8}$

one eighth $\frac{1}{8}$ | one eighth $\frac{1}{8}$

2) Match the fractions to make one whole:

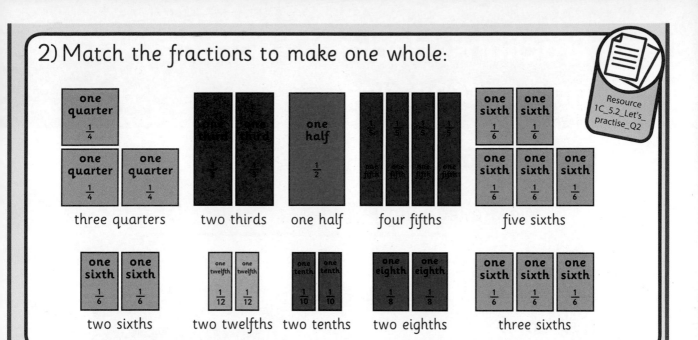

three quarters	two thirds

one half

four fifths

five sixths

two sixths

two twelfths

two tenths

two eighths

three sixths

★ **CHALLENGE!** ....

You will need:
- A fraction wall
- Scissors
- Glue

Isla has made one whole using the following:

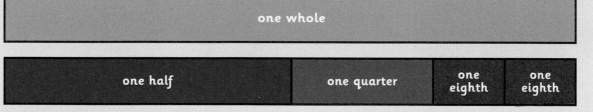

How many different ways can you make one whole using a mix of different fractions?

5 Fractions, decimal fractions and percentages

5.3 Ordering fractions

> We are learning to order simple fractions.

Before we start

Which is more?

a)   b)

> We can make and use fraction cards to order fractions by size.

Let's learn

Finlay has been asked to order these fractions from smallest to largest:

> Two is smaller than four and eight. One half must be the smallest.

one quarter	one half	one eighth
$\frac{1}{4}$	$\frac{1}{2}$	$\frac{1}{8}$

> I'm not sure that's right. Let's make the fractions with paper to check.

They make:

quarters

one quarter $\frac{1}{4}$	one quarter $\frac{1}{4}$
one quarter $\frac{1}{4}$	one quarter $\frac{1}{4}$

halves

one half $\frac{1}{2}$	one half $\frac{1}{2}$

eighths

one eighth $\frac{1}{8}$	one eighth $\frac{1}{8}$	one eighth $\frac{1}{8}$	one eighth $\frac{1}{8}$
one eighth $\frac{1}{8}$	one eighth $\frac{1}{8}$	one eighth $\frac{1}{8}$	one eighth $\frac{1}{8}$

Then cut out:

Now I can see that one eighth is the smallest because the whole has been split into more equal parts.

one quarter

one quarter
$\dfrac{1}{4}$

one half

one half
$\dfrac{1}{2}$

one eighth

one eighth
$\dfrac{1}{8}$

Now we can order them from smallest to largest:

one eighth

one eighth
$\dfrac{1}{8}$

one quarter

one quarter
$\dfrac{1}{4}$

one half

one half
$\dfrac{1}{2}$

Let's practise

1) Some of the fraction cards have lost their labels.
   Match the labels that are missing:

one whole

A

B

C

one eighth

D

E

F

G

one twelfth   one tenth

one half   one third

one fifth   one quarter

one sixth

2) Draw the labelled fraction cards in question 1 in the correct order from smallest to largest.

3) The children have mixed up their fraction labels.
Write them in order from largest to smallest:

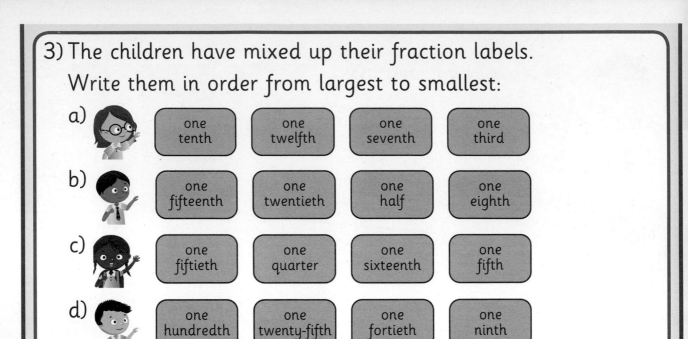

a)
| one tenth | one twelfth | one seventh | one third |

b)
| one fifteenth | one twentieth | one half | one eighth |

c)
| one fiftieth | one quarter | one sixteenth | one fifth |

d)
| one hundredth | one twenty-fifth | one fortieth | one ninth |

CHALLENGE!

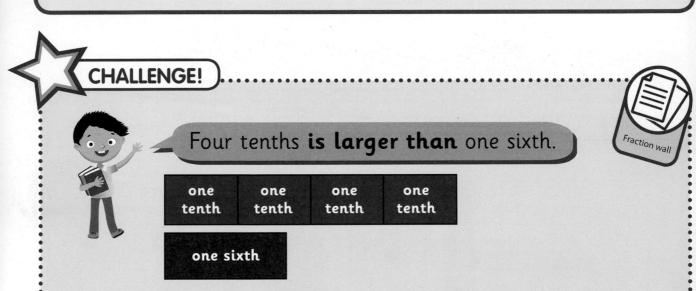

Four tenths **is larger than** one sixth.

| one tenth | one tenth | one tenth | one tenth |

| one sixth |

Fraction wall

Finlay uses a fraction wall to compare different fractions:

Compare some fractions by using the statements below. Use each statement at least twice.

• is larger than
• is smaller than
• is the same as

Ask a partner to check your statements.

5 Fractions, decimal fractions and percentages

5.4 Adding and subtracting fractions

We are learning to add and subtract fractions.

Before we start

Count how many:

one quarter $\frac{1}{4}$	one quarter $\frac{1}{4}$	one quarter $\frac{1}{4}$	one quarter $\frac{1}{4}$	one quarter $\frac{1}{4}$	one quarter $\frac{1}{4}$

one half $\frac{1}{2}$	one half $\frac{1}{2}$	one half $\frac{1}{2}$	one half $\frac{1}{2}$	one half $\frac{1}{2}$	one half $\frac{1}{2}$	one half $\frac{1}{2}$	one half $\frac{1}{2}$	one half $\frac{1}{2}$

We can add and subtract like fractions.

Let's learn

Finlay has three half cookies:

Amman has one half cookie:

How many do we have altogether?

Three halves plus one half is four half cookies altogether.

 =

3 halves + 1 half = 4 halves =   2 whole cookies

Four halves is exactly the same as two whole cookies.

Isla has three quarters of a cake:

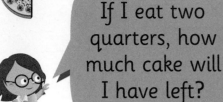
If I eat two quarters, how much cake will I have left?

3 quarters – 2 quarters = 1 quarter

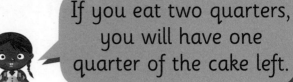
If you eat two quarters, you will have one quarter of the cake left.

Let's practise

1) How much do they have altogether?

a)

three half oranges　　+　　two half oranges　　=　　five half oranges

b)

five quarter cookies　　+　　four quarter cookies　　=　　_____ ?

c)

two thirds of a pizza　　+　　four thirds of a pizza　　=　　_____ ?

d)

four sixths　　+　　four sixths　　=　　_____ ?

e)

seven eighths　　+　　five eighths　　=　　_____ ?

2) How much will they each have left?

a)

four quarters

I am going to eat three quarters of a cookie.

b)

nine tenths

I am going to eat six tenths of a chocolate bar.

3) Solve the following problems. Think about how to show your thinking.

a) The football coach has 11 half oranges. Seven players eat a half orange at half-time. What does the coach have left?

b) Finlay has six tenths of a chocolate bar. Nuria has three tenths of a chocolate bar. How much chocolate do they have altogether?

c) Isla has five sixths of a pizza. Amman has four sixths of a pizza. They each give two sixths to Nuria. What do they have left?

CHALLENGE!

Work with a partner. You will need:

- fraction cards or tiles
- two sheets of card or paper

Take turns to choose some like fractions.

Hide some fraction cards under a sheet of paper and challenge your partner to work out how many you have hidden.

Fraction cards

5.5 Creating equivalent fractions

We are learning to create equivalent fractions using patterns.

Before we start

Match the fractions that are equal:

a)
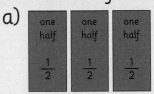

one half	one half	one half
$\frac{1}{2}$	$\frac{1}{2}$	$\frac{1}{2}$

three halves

b)

two thirds

c)

one sixth	one sixth
$\frac{1}{6}$	$\frac{1}{6}$
one sixth	one sixth
$\frac{1}{6}$	$\frac{1}{6}$

four sixths

d)

one quarter	one quarter	one quarter
$\frac{1}{4}$	$\frac{1}{4}$	$\frac{1}{4}$
one quarter	one quarter	one quarter
$\frac{1}{4}$	$\frac{1}{4}$	$\frac{1}{4}$

six quarters

We can find fractions that are equivalent by splitting them into equal parts.

Let's learn

Finlay thinks he has spotted a pattern to create fractions that are equal. He starts by making halves each time:

one half	one half

one half	one half

He splits halves into two equal parts to make quarters:

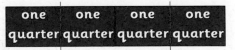

one quarter	one quarter	one quarter	one quarter

He splits halves into three equal parts to make sixths:

one sixth	one sixth	one sixth	one sixth	one sixth	one sixth

two halves is equal
to **four quarters**

one half is equal
to **two quarters**

two halves is equal
to **six sixths**

one half is equal
to **three sixths**

I can keep splitting my halves into more equal
parts to make more equivalent fractions.

Let's practise

1) Continue Finlay's pattern by splitting halves into:

a) Four equal parts:

one half	one half

↓

Two halves is equal to ____?____

One half is equal to ____?____

b) Five equal parts:

one half	one half

↓

Two halves is equal to ____?____

One half is equal to ____?____

c) Six equal parts:

one half	one half

↓

Two halves is equal to ____?____

One half is equal to ____?____

d) Seven equal parts:

one half	one half

↓

Two halves is equal to ____?____

One half is equal to ____?____

2) Split thirds into:

a) Two equal parts:

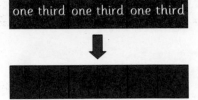

Three thirds is equal to _____?_____

One third is equal to _____?_____

b) Three equal parts:

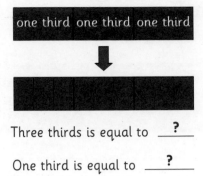

Three thirds is equal to _____?_____

One third is equal to _____?_____

c) Four equal parts:

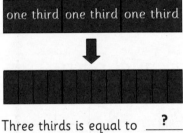

Three thirds is equal to _____?_____

One third is equal to _____?_____

d) Five equal parts:

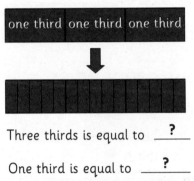

Three thirds is equal to _____?_____

One third is equal to _____?_____

CHALLENGE!

Amman has been asked to find fractions that are equivalent to:

- one quarter

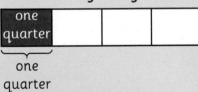

- two thirds

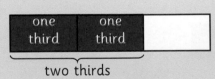

- three quarters

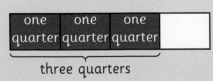

Find at least two equivalent fractions for each diagram.

Share your answers with a partner to check.

5.6 Comparing fractions

We are learning to compare fractions (relative to different wholes).

Before we start

Which is larger?

a)
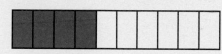

four fifths **or** four tenths

b)

two thirds **or** three sixths

When comparing fractions, it's important that we think about the size of the whole.

Let's learn

I think one half is always larger than one quarter.

one half | one half
one quarter | one quarter | one quarter | one quarter

That's true if we compare these two chocolate bars.

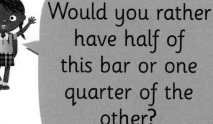
Would you rather have half of this bar or one quarter of the other?

one half | one half

one quarter | one quarter | one quarter | one quarter

The quarter is greater than the half portion. The bars are different sizes.

Finlay is wrong. One half is **always bigger** than one quarter if we are comparing objects **that are the same size**.

One half **can be smaller** than one quarter if we are comparing objects that are **different sizes**.

Let's practise

1) Which is larger?

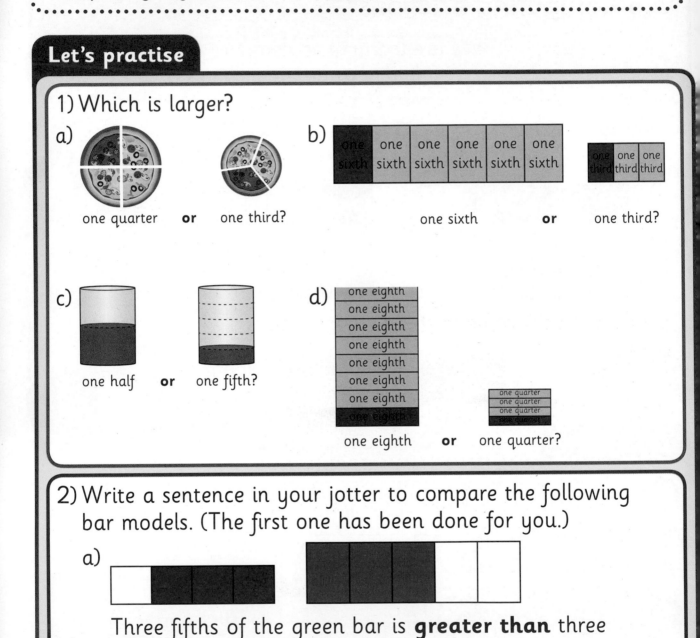

a) one quarter **or** one third?

b) one sixth   one sixth   one sixth   one sixth   one sixth   one sixth   one third   one third   one third

   one sixth   **or**   one third?

c) one half   **or**   one fifth?

d) one eighth one eighth one eighth one eighth one eighth one eighth one eighth one eighth   one quarter one quarter one quarter one quarter

   one eighth   **or**   one quarter?

2) Write a sentence in your jotter to compare the following bar models. (The first one has been done for you.)

a)

Three fifths of the green bar is **greater than** three quarters of the red bar.

b)

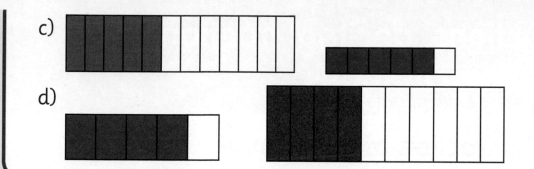

c)

d)

3) Draw diagrams to prove that:

a) One fifth **can be greater than** one third.

b) One half **can be smaller than** one sixth.

c) Two quarters **can be larger than** two thirds.

d) Four fifths **can be smaller than** four tenths.

★ CHALLENGE!

Chocolate bars come in three different sizes:

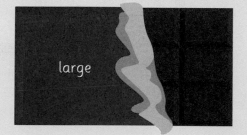

The lengths of each side double from small to medium and from medium to large.

Finlay is offered:

• five small bars, OR

• one and a half medium bars, OR

• one quarter of a large bar.

Which option should he choose to get the most chocolate? Can you prove it?

5.7 Find a fraction of an amount

We are learning to solve fraction problems using division and multiplication.

Before we start

Solve:

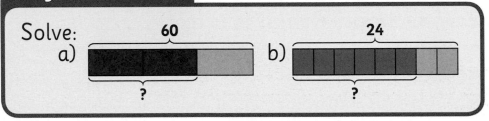

a) 60 ?

b) 24 ?

We can find a fraction of a value using division and multiplication.

Let's learn

Nuria receives £30 for her birthday:

I am going to spend **two-thirds** of my birthday money on a new bag.

We can solve this using a bar model:

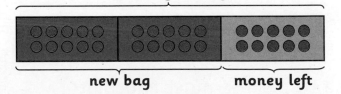

birthday money

new bag   money left

Two thirds of **£30** = **£20**   The bag costs **£20**.

We can use another strategy to solve this:

When we share the birthday money between each third we are dividing by 3.

When we find how much the bag costs, we are multiplying the £10 by 2.

£30 ÷ 3 = £10   **£10 × 2 = £20**

So, to work out two thirds of £30 we can:

Divide by the denominator   **then**   multiply by the numerator

$\frac{2}{3}$ of **£30**   =   £30 ÷ 3 = £10
                              then £10 × 2 = £20

Or, we can do it the other way round:

Multiply by the numerator
          then $\frac{2}{3}$ of **£30**   =   £30 × 2 = £60
divide by the denominator   **then** £60 ÷ 3 = £20

Let's practise

1) Solve the following using division and multiplication (the first one has been done for you):

a)
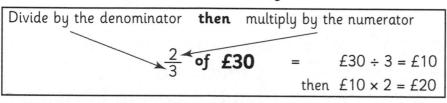
27

?

$\frac{2}{3}$ of 27 :   27 ÷ 3 = 9
                        9 × 2 = **18**

b)

32

?

$\frac{3}{4}$ of 32 : $\frac{?\ =\ ?}{?\ =\ ?}$

c)
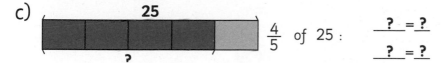
25

?

$\frac{4}{5}$ of 25 : $\frac{?\ =\ ?}{?\ =\ ?}$

d)
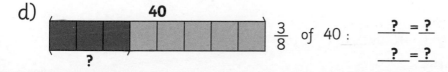
40

?

$\frac{3}{8}$ of 40 : $\frac{?\ =\ ?}{?\ =\ ?}$

2) Solve:

a) $\frac{3}{4}$ of 36 apples = **?**

b) $\frac{5}{6}$ of 30 oranges = **?**

c) $\frac{7}{10}$ of 90 grapes = **?**

d) $\frac{3}{7}$ of 21 cherries = **?**

3) Write number stories for each of the following:

a) A bus has **42 seats**. The bus is **five-sixths** full. How many people are on the bus?

b) Finlay is reading a book with **60 pages**. He's read **eight-tenths** of the book. How much has he read?

c) Nuria is on a train travelling from Glasgow to Edinburgh. She is **two-thirds** of the way there. The journey lasts **45 minutes**. How long has she been travelling so far?

CHALLENGE!

Make up word problems for the following bar models:

a)
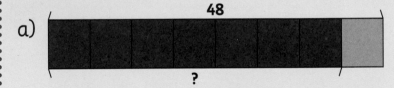
48
?

b)
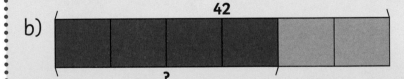
42
?

c)
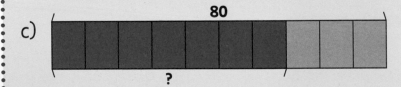
80
?

Demonstrate how you would solve these using division and multiplication.

5.8 Sharing one whole

We are learning to share one whole and record findings.

Before we start

How much more do each of the children need to make one whole?

a)

one half $\frac{1}{2}$

b)

one sixth $\frac{1}{6}$	one sixth $\frac{1}{6}$
one sixth $\frac{1}{6}$	one sixth $\frac{1}{6}$

c)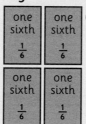

one tenth $\frac{1}{10}$	one tenth $\frac{1}{10}$	one tenth $\frac{1}{10}$
one tenth $\frac{1}{10}$	one tenth $\frac{1}{10}$	one tenth $\frac{1}{10}$

d)

one eighth $\frac{1}{8}$	
one eighth $\frac{1}{8}$	one eighth $\frac{1}{8}$

We can use bar models to show how one whole can be split into equal parts.

Let's learn

The children want to share the cake equally between them:

We will need to cut it into four equal parts.

We can represent this using a bar model:

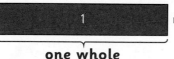

1

⟹

one quarter	one quarter	one quarter	one quarter

one whole   four quarters

Isla, Nuria, Amman and Finlay will each get one quarter of the cake.

One whole shared between **four** = **one quarter** each.

Nuria and Amman are sharing this pizza:

I only want two sixths of the pizza.

How much will be left for me?

| 1 | | | → | one sixth | one sixth | one sixth | one sixth | one sixth | one sixth |

one whole   Nuria   Amman

Amman will be left with **four sixths** of the pizza.

Let's practise

1) Draw bar models to solve how much **each person** will get:

   a) One pizza is to be shared equally between six people.
   b) One chocolate bar is to be shared between eight people.
   c) One bottle of orange juice is to be shared between three people.
   d) One cake is to be shared between 12 people.

2) Finlay and Isla are sharing out food:

Isla is going to take:
   · **one quarter** of the cookie
   · **seven tenths** of the chocolate bar
   · **three eighths** of the pizza
   · **one third** of the orange juice
   · **one sixth** of the cake

What's left for me?

Draw bar models to show how much Finlay will get (the first one is done for you):

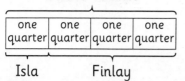
whole cookie

one quarter	one quarter	one quarter	one quarter

Isla   Finlay

Finlay will get **three-quarters** of the cookie.

⭐ CHALLENGE!

The bar models show how Isla, Amman and Nuria are going to share out the following:

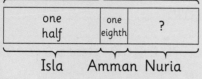
whole cookie

one half	one eighth	?

Isla   Amman   Nuria

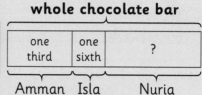
whole chocolate bar

one third	one sixth	?

Amman   Isla   Nuria

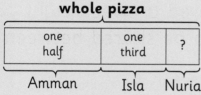
whole pizza

one half	one third	?

Amman   Isla   Nuria

What fraction of each will Nuria get?

6.1 Recording amounts

> We are learning to record amounts of money using decimal notation.

Before we start

Nuria and Finlay are trying to make £6 and 74p.
Nuria says she can make it using one note and four coins.
Finlay says he will need at least one note and five coins.
What do you think? Explain your thinking.

> We can record amounts in different ways.

Let's learn

This amount is £6 and 43p. This is the same as 643p.

We can also record this amount in decimal notation as £6.43.

> Take care:
> £3 and 5p is written £3.05 in decimal notation.
>
> £3 and 50p is written £3.50 (*never* £3.5).

The **pounds (£)** are before the decimal point and the **pence (p)** are after the decimal point.

Let's practise

1) a) Write these amounts in £ and p:

   i) £15.10   ii) £28.11   iii) £14.09   iv) £2.99

   b) Write these amounts in decimal notation:

   i) £12 and 15p   ii) £30 and 30p
   iii) £7 and 8p   iv) £19 and 70p

   c) Draw the smallest number of notes and coins that makes each amount.

2) Write down these amounts in decimal notation.

   a)

   b)

   c)

   d)

3) Use the least notes and coins you can to make these amounts.

   Draw the notes and coins you choose.
   a) £9.80   b) £35.25   c) £20.99   d) £15.07

⭐ CHALLENGE!

Amman has two hundred pounds. Nuria gives him another one pound and fifty-six pence. Write down the amount Amman has now, using decimal notation.

Draw Amman's new amount, using the smallest number of notes (no larger than £20) and coins you can.

6.2 Adding amounts

We are learning to add amounts up to £10.

Before we start

Isla buys two cartons of milk at 35p each.

In her purse, she has these coins:

What is the smallest number of coins she can use to pay?

Adding amounts helps us to check that we have enough money.

Let's learn

Money, or cash, is not the only way we can pay for things.

If someone uses a debit card, bank transfer or a PayPal account, the money comes straight out of their bank account. So, although no coins or notes are given, the money is still spent.

If you are given a gift card, you need to be sure you have enough money on it to pay for the things you want.

When shopping, we can add the cost of items as we go along. This way we don't go to the checkout with more items than we can afford.

1) The children each have some cash.
   Finlay's money:

   Nuria's money:

   Isla's money:

   a) Write down how much money each child has, using digital notation.
   b) How much money do Finlay and Nuria have in total?
   c) How much money do Nuria and Isla have in total?
   d) How much money do Finlay and Isla have in total?
   e) How much money do the three children have altogether?
   Draw the amount using the least amount of coins.

2) Nuria is in the supermarket with her mum. They buy bread, milk, cheese and eggs.

   £1.25   85p   £2.15   £1.20

   Nuria's mum wants to pay by debit card. She has £5 in the bank. How much more money does she need to be able to buy all the items?

3) Finlay's dad has £8.50 in his bank account. He goes online to buy some books using his PayPal account. He chooses three books, each costing £2.70. Does he have enough money in his account to pay for the books?

4) The children have been given £10 each to buy equipment for school. They go to the shop:

Calculator	Pen	Colouring pens	Colouring pencils	Pencil sharpener	Maths set	Rubber	Scissors
£8.75	£2.50	£5.10	£4.25	£1.20	£1.75	80p	£3.40

- Finlay wants a calculator and a maths set.
- Nuria wants scissors, colouring pens and a pencil sharpener.
- Isla wants colouring pencils, a pen and scissors.
- Amman wants a maths set, scissors and colouring pens.
  a) Add the amounts to calculate whether each child has enough money to buy the things they want.
  b) i) If they have enough money, calculate how much they would have left from £10.
     ii) If they don't have enough, calculate how much more money they need.

⭐ **CHALLENGE!**

Amman is in a fast food restaurant. He is allowed to spend up to £8. He can buy up to three items, but is only allowed either fizzy juice or ice-cream, not both.

a) Which combinations of food can he afford to buy?

b) If Amman buys the most expensive combination of food he can afford, how much money will he have left over?

c) How much will he have left over if he buys the cheapest combination?

 £3.19
£1.80
 £2.79
£1.99
 £3.89
 £2.59

6.3 Calculating change

We are learning to calculate change.

Before we start

500p – 229p = ?

What strategy would you use? Talk to a partner.

When we calculate change, we usually count on.

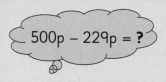

Let's learn

Amman is paying for items that cost £8.56 with a £10 note.

He calculates his change.

He counts on from £8.56:

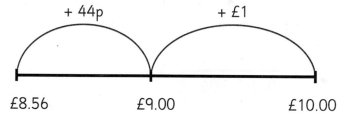

+ 44p   + £1

£8.56   £9.00   £10.00

His change is £1.44. Now he can check that the shopkeeper gives him the right amount.

**Let's practise**

1) Calculate the change from the notes given for items that cost

a) £6.50   b) £7.25   c) £1.80

£10   £20   £5

d) £6.33

e) £0.91

2) Finlay and Nuria buy computer games. Draw the coins and notes they each get as change using the least number of coins.

a) Finlay buys a game that costs £7.75 and pays with a £10 note.

b) Nuria buys one that costs £6.89. She pays with a £20 note.

3) The children are at the supermarket. They each have a £10 note.

| £1.50 | £2.75 | £3.00 | £1.97 | £1.09 | £1.58 | 95p | £1.99 |

Finlay buys

Nuria buys

Amman buys

Isla buys

Find the total cost of the items for each child.

a) Calculate their change from £10.

b) Draw the notes and coins they will receive in change, using the least amount of coins.

Isla is buying nail varnish. If she buys four, she gets 25p off.
She buys four nail varnishes at £1.75 each.

a) How much does she need to pay?

b) She has these notes and coins in her purse:

Can she pay with the right money?

c) She decides to pay with the £5 note and the £2 coin. How much change does she receive?

Buy 4, get 25p off

7.1 Use a calendar to plan events

> We are learning to use a calendar to plan events.

Before we start

With a partner, record a list of important dates for the month – include birthdays, trips, activities and clubs.

Day   Date   Event

> A **calendar** is used to *plan*, *record* and *measure* time.

Let's learn

There are many different ways that time can be recorded and measured.

JANUARY

S	M	T	W	T	F	S
		1	2	3	4	5
6	7	8	9	10	11	12
13	14	15	16	17	18	19
20	21	22	23	24	25	26
27	28	29	30	31		

FEBRUARY

S	M	T	W	T	F	S
					1	2
3	4	5	6	7	8	9
10	11	12	13	14	15	16
17	18	19	20	21	22	23
24	25	26	27	28		

MARCH

S	M	T	W	T	F	S
					1	2
3	4	5	6	7	8	9
10	11	12	13	14	15	16
17	18	19	20	21	22	23
24	25	26	27	28	29	30
31						

APRIL

S	M	T	W	T	F	S
	1	2	3	4	5	6
7	8	9	10	11	12	13
14	15	16	17	18	19	20
21	22	23	24	25	26	27
28	29	30				

MAY

S	M	T	W	T	F	S
			1	2	3	4
5	6	7	8	9	10	11
12	13	14	15	16	17	18
19	20	21	22	23	24	25
26	27	28	29	30	31	

JUNE

S	M	T	W	T	F	S
						1
2	3	4	5	6	7	8
9	10	11	12	13	14	15
16	17	18	19	20	21	22
23	24	25	26	27	28	29
30						

JULY

S	M	T	W	T	F	S
	1	2	3	4	5	6
7	8	9	10	11	12	13
14	15	16	17	18	19	20
21	22	23	24	25	26	27
28	29	30	31			

AUGUST

S	M	T	W	T	F	S
				1	2	3
4	5	6	7	8	9	10
11	12	13	14	15	16	17
18	19	20	21	22	23	24
25	26	27	28	29	30	31

SEPTEMBER

S	M	T	W	T	F	S
1	2	3	4	5	6	7
8	9	10	11	12	13	14
15	16	17	18	19	20	21
22	23	24	25	26	27	28
29	30					

OCTOBER

S	M	T	W	T	F	S
		1	2	3	4	5
6	7	8	9	10	11	12
13	14	15	16	17	18	19
20	21	22	23	24	25	26
27	28	29	30	31		

NOVEMBER

S	M	T	W	T	F	S
					1	2
3	4	5	6	7	8	9
10	11	12	13	14	15	16
17	18	19	20	21	22	23
24	25	26	27	28	29	30

DECEMBER

S	M	T	W	T	F	S
1	2	3	4	5	6	7
8	9	10	11	12	13	14
15	16	17	18	19	20	21
22	23	24	25	26	27	28
29	30	31				

Using a **calendar**, you can look at a **week**, **month** and **year**.

Let's practise

1) Look at the calendar and answer the following questions:

   a) What day is the 14th of March?
   b) What date is the last Sunday of March?
   c) What day is the 1st of March?

MARCH

S	M	T	W	T	F	S
					1	2
3	4	5	6	7	8	9
10	11	12	13	14	15	16
17	18	19	20	21	22	23
24	25	26	27	28	29	30
31						

2) Look at the calendar and answer the following questions:

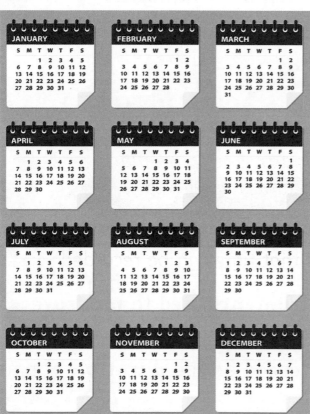

a) What day is the 15th of June?

b) What is the date of the first Monday in August?

c) Write the date of the second Tuesday in January using words and numbers.

Resource 1C_7.1_Let's_practise_Q2

⭐ **CHALLENGE!** ....

With a partner, create a monthly calendar that has the dates of all the birthdays in your class.

Add in any other important dates including:

- School holidays
- Sports day

7.2 Recording time

We are learning to use a variety of timers to record events.

Before we start

Can you name the following ways to measure time?

a)

b)

c)

d)

Time periods can be recorded using different instruments.

Let's learn

There are many different **instruments** used to **measure** periods of **time**.

The instrument you use will depend on the **duration** of time you are measuring.

1) Select the appropriate instrument for each of these activities:
   a) running a race
   b) planning a holiday
   c) brushing your teeth
   d) watching a film
   e) cooking a pizza
   f) taking a maths test

2) With a partner, use a stopwatch to time the following activities. Record the times in your jotters:
   a) clap your hands 20 times
   b) stand up and sit down 10 times
   c) draw 10 squares
   d) say your name 15 times
   e) write out the multiplication facts for five
   f) throw and catch a ball 10 times

CHALLENGE!

Work with a partner to research an instrument that measures time. Record the following details:
✓ name of time-measuring instrument
✓ unit of time it measures
✓ when it was invented
✓ who invented it
✓ what it is used for
Create a display to show your findings.

7.3 Convert digital to analogue

We are learning to convert between digital and analogue time.

Before we start

Using a clock face, show your partner the following times:

a) 11 : 30   b) 9 : 15   c) 4 : 00   d) 2 : 45

Analogue clocks and digital clocks both represent the time.

Let's learn

An **analogue** clock is a clock with the numbers 1 to 12 around the outside, a shorter hand to measure hours and a longer hand to measure minutes.

A **digital** clock is a clock that simply shows numbers to represent the time.

Let's practise

1) Copy and complete the sentence and circle am or pm.

   a) I wake up at [?] am / pm.

   b) I arrive at school at [?] am / pm.

   c) I have lunch at [?] am / pm.

   d) I get ready for bed at [?] am / pm.

2) Match the clocks and watches that are showing the same time.

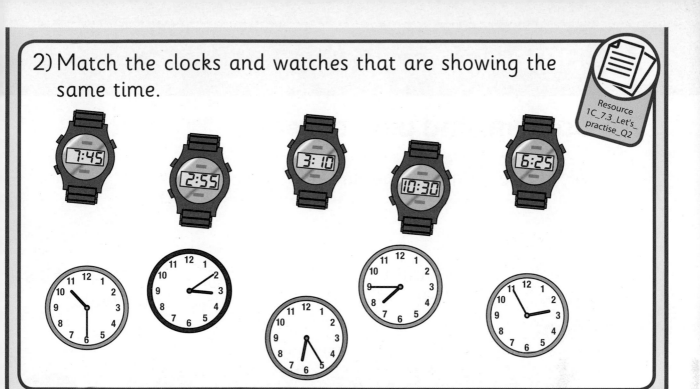

Resource 1C_7.3_Let's_practise_Q2

CHALLENGE!

Here is a timeline for William. Create your own timeline about you.

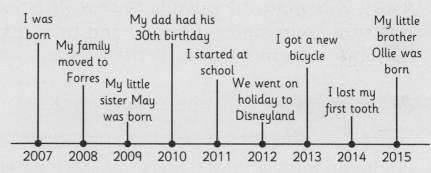

I was born

My family moved to Forres

My little sister May was born

My dad had his 30th birthday

I started at school

We went on holiday to Disneyland

I got a new bicycle

I lost my first tooth

My little brother Ollie was born

2007 2008 2009 2010 2011 2012 2013 2014 2015

Construct your school day as a timeline, broken down into blocks of 15 minutes. Include your school starting time, break time, lunch time and maths lesson.

a) How many minutes is it between the start of the day and lunch time?

b) How many minutes does the whole day last for?

c) Write your own school day questions for your partner to answer.

7.4 Use a.m. and p.m. correctly

> We are learning to use a.m. and p.m. correctly.

Before we start

List three things you would do in the morning, three things you would do in the afternoon and three things you would do at night.

> A 12-hour digital clock uses **a.m**. and **p.m**. to indicate morning and afternoon/evening.

Let's learn

Ante meridiem or **a.m**. is the time before midday.

Post meridiem or **p.m.** is the time after midday.

Let's practise

Blank clock faces

1) For the following activities, indicate whether they would be a.m., p.m. or both:
   a) having breakfast
   b) eating dinner
   c) getting dressed for school
   d) going to bed
   e) brushing your teeth
   f) walking to school

2) Write a.m. or p.m. next to each time in your jotter and draw an analogue clock to show the same time.
   a) 04 : 30
   b) 12 : 50
   c) 18 : 00
   d) 00 : 10
   e) 14 : 45
   f) 07 : 20

Nuria woke up at 6:00 a.m. She looked at the time on different clocks until she had lunch at 2:00 p.m.

Resource 1C_ 7.4_Challenge

a) Number the pictures from 2 to 8 to show the correct order she saw the clocks.

1		(a.m)/ p.m
?		a.m / p.m
?		a.m / p.m
?		a.m / p.m
?		a.m / p.m

? a.m / p.m

? a.m / p.m

? a.m / p.m

b) Circle 'a.m.' or 'p.m.' next to each clock.

7.5 12-hour and 24-hour time

We are learning to use 12-hour and 24-hour time.

Before we start

What is the difference between 12-hour and 24-hour time?

Time can be represented in 12-hour or 24-hour notation.

Let's learn

The 24-hour clock is the time shown as how many hours and minutes since midnight.

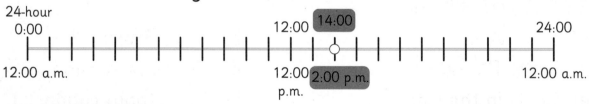

Let's practise

1) Copy and complete the following charts. Write next to each time what you would normally be doing at this time.

Resource 1C_7.5_Let's practise_Q1

00:00	12 midnight	12:00	12 noon
?	01:00 a.m.	?	1:00 p.m.
02:00	02:00 a.m.	14:00	?
03:00	?	15:00	3:00 p.m.
04:00	04:00 a.m.	?	4:00 p.m.
05:00	05:00 a.m.	?	5:00 p.m.
?	06:00 a.m.	18:00	?
07:00	?	19:00	7:00 p.m.
08:00	08:00 a.m.	?	8:00 p.m.
09:00	?	21:00	?
10:00	10:00 a.m.	?	10:00 p.m.
?	11:00 a.m.	23:00	?

2) Use the timetable to answer the following:

Departures

Time	To/Via
08:20	LONDON
09:05	BARCELONA
09:30	MOSCOW
10:20	PARIS
10:45	ROME
11:10	BERLIN

a) Are the flights a.m. or p.m.?

b) The next flight to Rome departs at 14:00, how long is there between flights to Rome?

c) The flight to London will take 1 hour 30 minutes. What time will it arrive?

3) This is the timetable for two television stations.

What time are the following programmes on? Answer using 12-hour clock times.

Leckie Channel	City 7 TV
17.00 – Smallville	17.30 – News
18.00 – Cartoons	18.00 – Weather
18.30 – Peeta Planet	18.15 – Basil Brush
19.00 – News	18.45 – Heartbreak High
19.30 – Weather	19.00 – Chefs in the City

a) Smallville

b) Basil Brush

c) Peeta Planet

d) Heartbreak High

e) Chefs in the City

f) News (both channels)

CHALLENGE!

Resource 1C_7.5_Challenge

Flights depart from Inverness International Airport to Bristol every 45 minutes. The flight takes 1 hour 50 minutes. The flight stops for 15 minutes to refuel and pick up passengers and then returns to Inverness. Use this information to fill in the timetable.

Departure times	7.00	7.45	8.30	9.15	10.00
Arrive Bristol	8.50				
Depart	9.05				
Arrive Inverness	10.55				

How often can the same plane be used to make the journey to Bristol and back in eight hours?

8.1 Reading and recording measurements – length

We are learning to read and record measurements to simple fractions (length).

Before we start

How long is each line?

a)

b)

We can measure length and height more accurately by reading measurements using fractions.

Let's learn

The end of this line is exactly halfway between 1 and 2 cm.

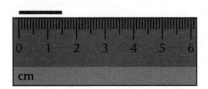

We can say it measures **one and a half centimetres**.

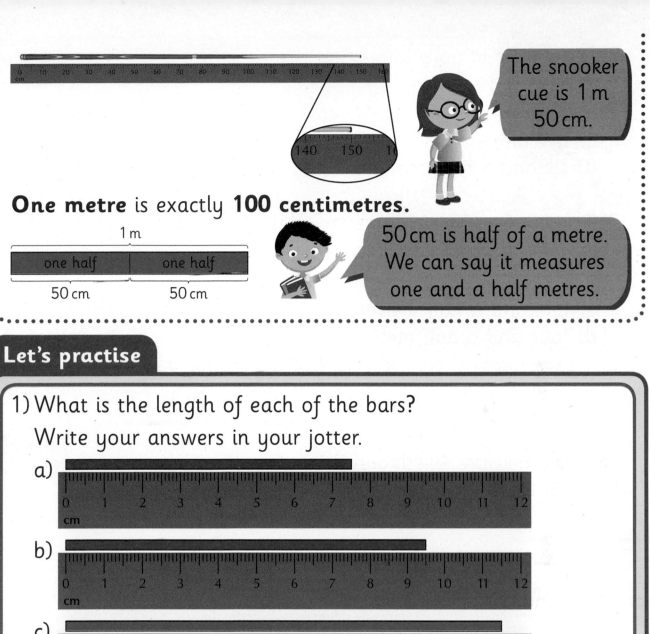

The snooker cue is 1 m 50 cm.

One metre is exactly **100 centimetres.**

1 m

one half	one half
50 cm	50 cm

50 cm is half of a metre. We can say it measures one and a half metres.

Let's practise

1) What is the length of each of the bars?
Write your answers in your jotter.

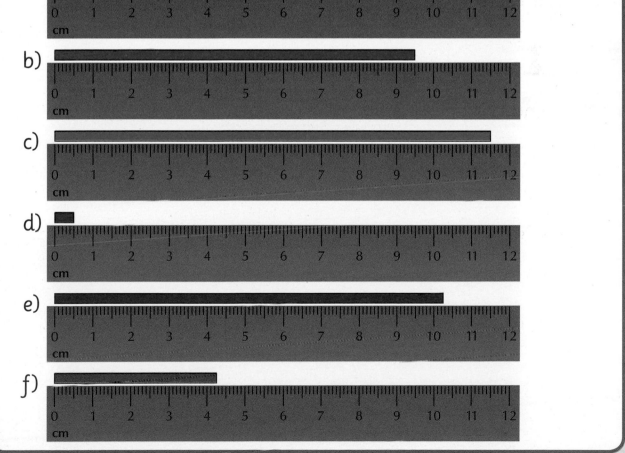

a)

b)

c)

d)

e)

f)

2) Draw lines in your jotter that are exactly:

   a) two and a half centimetres
   b) seven and a half centimetres
   c) five and a half centimetres
   d) six and a half centimetres

3) Draw lines in the playground that are exactly:

   a) three and a half metres
   b) six and a half metres
   c) one and a half metres
   d) four and a half metres

CHALLENGE!

Resource 1C_
8.1_Challenge

Nuria has been asked to draw lines that are 6 cm, 10 cm, 12 cm, 15 cm and 20 cm. Here are her attempts:

a) $3\frac{1}{2}$ cm ☐

b) $5\frac{1}{2}$ cm ☐

c) $7\frac{1}{2}$ cm ☐

d) $9\frac{1}{2}$ cm ☐

e) $11\frac{1}{4}$ cm ☐

Amman helps by completing the first line to 6 cm:

$3\frac{1}{2}$ cm $2\frac{1}{2}$ cm

Copy each of the lines above and finish them off using a different colour.

8 Measurement

8.2 Measuring and recording length – millimetres

We are learning to measure and record length in millimetres.

Before we start

Use a ruler to measure the length of each bar:

a)

b)

Millimetres are often used in jobs where accuracy is very important, such as the building trade.

Let's learn

'Centi' means 'one hundredth'. There are 100 centimetres in a metre.

100 centimetres

one metre

1000 millimetres

'Milli' means 'one thousandth'. There are 1000 millimetres in a metre.

The lines between each centimetre on a ruler show millimetres.

There are 10 millimetres (mm) in a centimetre (cm).

This ruler shows centimetres:

1 cm = 10 mm

This ruler shows millimetres:

This line measures 23 mm.

Let's practise

1) What is the length of each of the bars?
   Write your answers in your jotter.

a)
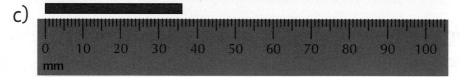

b)

c)
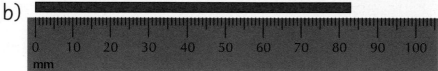

d)
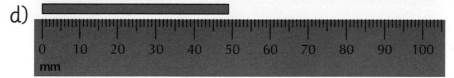

e)

f)

2) Measure the height of each of the characters below (to the nearest millimetre):

a)
b)
c)
d)

3) Draw lines that are exactly:

a) 8 millimetres
b) 13 millimetres
c) 30 millimetres
d) 45 millimetres
e) 78 millimetres
f) 99 millimetres

CHALLENGE!

Choose two items from your classroom that measure between:

· 1 mm and 100 mm
· 100 mm and 200 mm
· 200 mm and 300 mm

Measure them to the nearest millimetre and record your measurements.

8.3 Converting length – millimetres and centimetres

We are learning to convert standard units of length (mm, cm).

Before we start

Write the following measurements in another way:

a) 2 m 57 cm   b) 309 cm   c) 5 m 5 cm

We can state measurements in either millimetres or centimetres.

Let's learn

This line is 4 cm long.

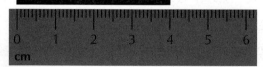

We know that each centimetre is equal to 10 millimetres. The line is 40 mm long.

We can convert centimetres into millimetres: **4 cm = 40 mm**.

This line is 25 mm.

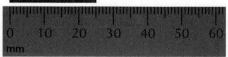

We can also say the line is 2 cm and 5 mm long (or two and a half centimetres).

We can convert millimetres into centimetres: **25 mm = 2 cm** and **5 mm = 2$\frac{1}{2}$ cm**.

1) Convert the following measurements into millimetres:

a)
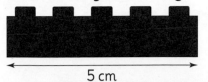
5 cm

b)

6 cm

c)
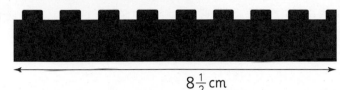
$8\frac{1}{2}$ cm

d)
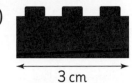
3 cm

2) Convert the following measurements into centimetres and millimetres (the first one has been done for you):
a) 82 mm = 8 cm and 2 mm
b) 55 mm   c) 47 mm   d) 23 mm
e) 76 mm   f) 110 mm   g) 134 mm

3) Measure each of the bars and state their length in two ways:
a)
b)
c)
d)
e)
f)

⭐ CHALLENGE!

You will need:

· string   · scissors   · ruler

I choose 78 mm.

With a partner, take turns choosing a measurement in millimetres. Without using the ruler to help, try to cut a piece of string to the chosen length. Measure each of your attempts. Closest wins a point. First to four wins!

8.4 Reading and recording measurements for mass

We are learning to read and record measurements to simple fractions (mass).

Before we start

How much do they each have?

a)

b)

c)

We can measure mass more accurately by reading measurements using fractions.

Let's learn

The scales are exactly halfway between 1 kg and 2 kg.

We can say the bag weighs **one and a half kilograms.**

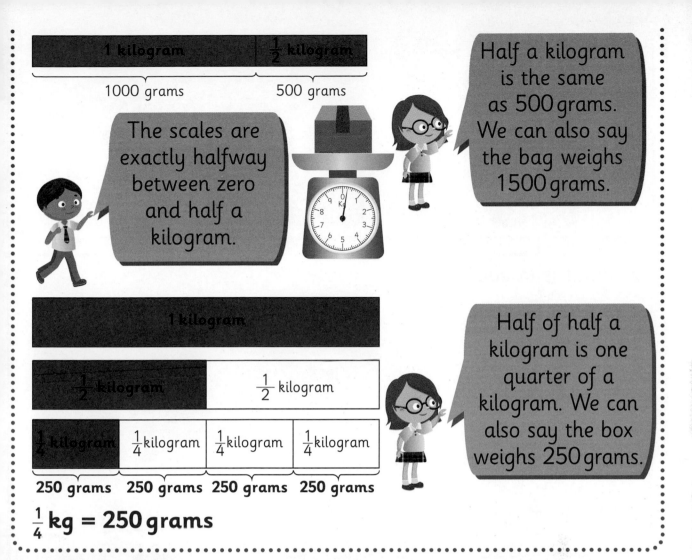

1 kilogram | ½ kilogram

1000 grams | 500 grams

The scales are exactly halfway between zero and half a kilogram.

Half a kilogram is the same as 500 grams. We can also say the bag weighs 1500 grams.

1 kilogram

½ kilogram | ½ kilogram

¼ kilogram | ¼ kilogram | ¼ kilogram | ¼ kilogram

250 grams | 250 grams | 250 grams | 250 grams

Half of half a kilogram is one quarter of a kilogram. We can also say the box weighs 250 grams.

$\frac{1}{4}$ **kg = 250 grams**

Let's practise

1) What is the mass of the following (state your answer in kilograms)?

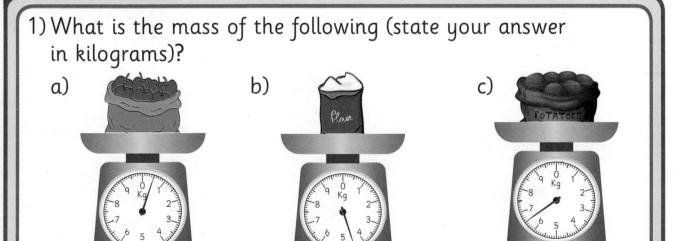

a)

b)

c)

d)   e)   f)

2) What is in each box?

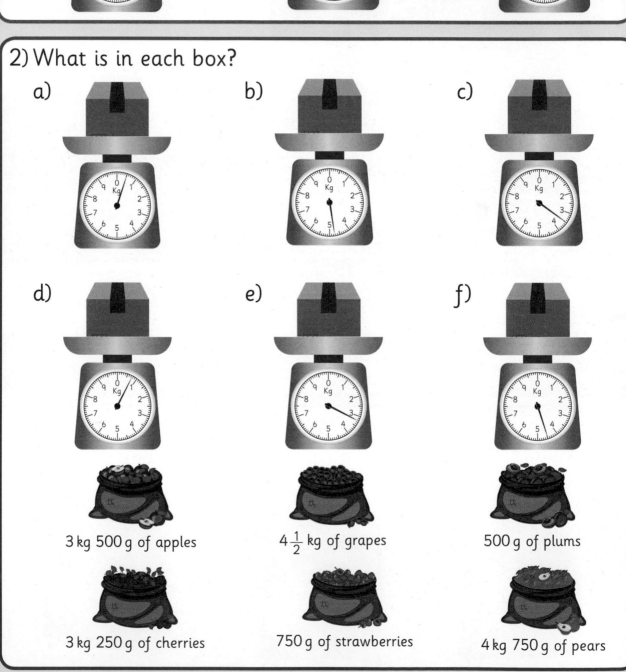

a)   b)   c)

d)   e)   f)

3 kg 500 g of apples   4 $\frac{1}{2}$ kg of grapes   500 g of plums

3 kg 250 g of cherries   750 g of strawberries   4 kg 750 g of pears

3) Draw the scales for each of the following weights (the first one has been done for you):

a)

b)

c)

d)

e)

⭐ CHALLENGE!

You will need:

- a box or bag
- kitchen scales
- small items to be weighed

Fill the box (or bag) to make the following measurements:

a) $\frac{1}{2}$ kg   b) $1\frac{1}{2}$ kg   c) $2\frac{1}{2}$ kg   d) $\frac{1}{4}$ kg   e) $1\frac{3}{4}$ kg

Share your results by taking a photograph of your scales.

The mass of the potatoes is **1 kg 12 g**.

The capacity of the bottle is **2 l** or **2000 ml**.

Let's practise

1) Convert the following lengths:

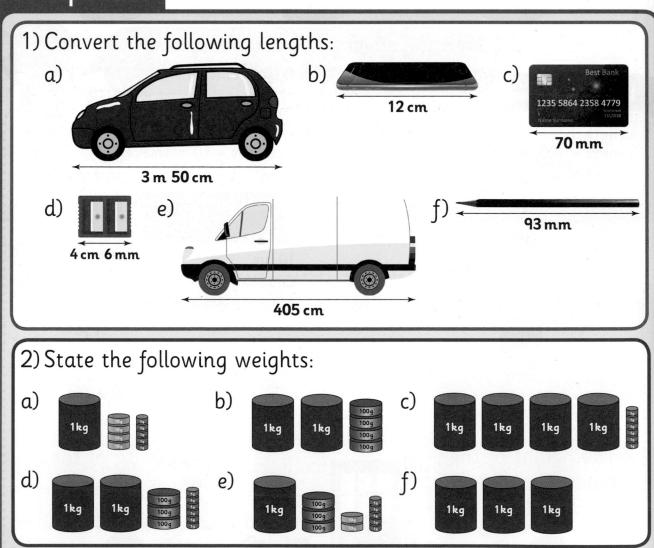

a) **3 m 50 cm**

b) **12 cm**

c) **70 mm**

d) **4 cm 6 mm**

e) **405 cm**

f) **93 mm**

2) State the following weights:

a) 1kg 10g 10g 10g 10g 1g 1g 1g 1g

b) 1kg 1kg 100g 100g 100g 100g

c) 1kg 1kg 1kg 1kg 1g 1g 1g 1g 1g 1g

d) 1kg 1kg 100g 100g 100g 1g 1g 1g 1g

e) 1kg 100g 100g 100g 10g 10g 1g 1g 1g 1g

f) 1kg 1kg 1kg

3) Convert the following volumes:

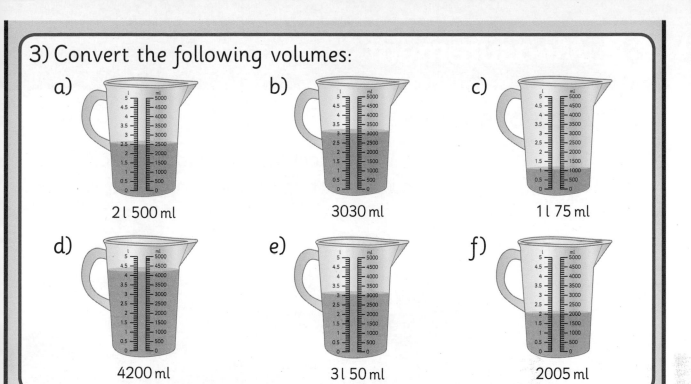

a) 2 l 500 ml

b) 3030 ml

c) 1 l 75 ml

d) 4200 ml

e) 3 l 50 ml

f) 2005 ml

⭐ **CHALLENGE!** ....

You will need:
- 2-litre bottle
- measuring tape
- scales
- measuring jug

a) Fill the bottle with water (between half and full).
b) Measure the height of the water level.
c) Measure the weight of the bottle.
d) Measure the volume of water.
e) State each of the above measurements in two
  different ways.

8.7 Area of shapes

We are learning to read and record measurements of area including half squares.

Before we start

What is the area of these shapes?

a)  b) 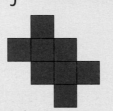 c)

We can use half squares to measure the area of different shapes accurately.

Let's learn

Nuria and Finlay have been asked to measure the area of this shape:

Let's use square tiles to help us.

There isn't enough space to fit another square.

We can cut the square into two equal parts to make half squares.

We can cover the spaces with the two half squares.

The children can fit six squares and two half squares on top of the shape.

The **area** of the shape is **seven squares**.

Let's practise

1) What is the area of the following shapes?

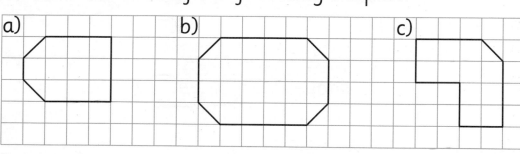

a)   b)   c)

Squared paper

2) Estimate how many 1 cm squares will fit on each shape:

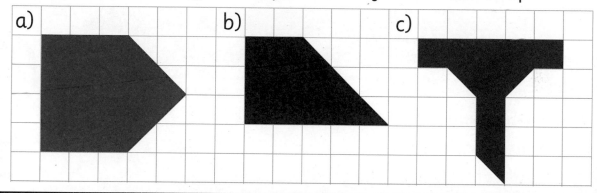

a)   b)   c)

3) Use squared paper to make and measure the area for each of the shapes in question 2.

CHALLENGE!

Finlay estimates the area of shape A to be 24 squares by matching parts of squares that he thinks will make a whole square altogether.

Estimate the area of shapes B and C:

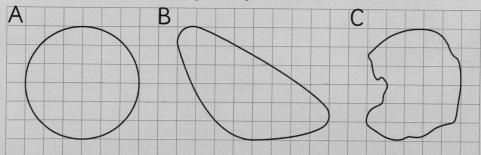

A   B   C

8.8 Creating areas

We are learning to create shapes with a specified area.

Before we start

Draw shapes that have an area of:
a) 8 squares   b) $10\frac{1}{2}$ squares

We can design shapes that have the same area but a different appearance.

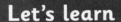

Amman has been asked to create shapes using these tiles:

He arranges them to make different shapes:

All of these shapes have an area of 10 squares.

We can cut some of the squares into two equal parts to make half squares.

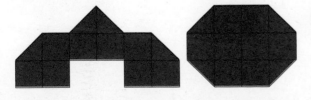

Now we can make even more shapes with an area of 10 squares.

These shapes both use eight whole squares and four half squares, making 10 squares altogether.

1) Use squared paper to draw two shapes that have the same area as each of the following shapes:

a)    b)   c)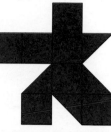

Squared paper

2) Use 12 tiles like these to create each of the following:

a) A shape with at least one side that is three squares long.
b) A shape with two sides that are exactly four squares long.
c) A shape where no two sides are the same length.
d) A shape with 10 sides.

3) Use squared paper to design shapes that have an area of:
a) Nine squares (whole squares only)
b) $13\frac{1}{2}$ squares
c) 16 squares (must include four half squares)
d) $19\frac{1}{2}$ squares (must include more than three half squares)

CHALLENGE!

You will need:

• eight whole squares

• eight half squares

Isla has used whole and half squares to make the number 8.

How many numbers and letters can you make using exactly the same number of tiles?

8.9 Area and arrays

We are learning to calculate area using arrays.

Before we start

Draw an array making a total of:
a) 15   b) 18

Arrays can help us calculate the area of rectangles and squares.

Let's learn

We can calculate the area of this rectangle by counting the squares:

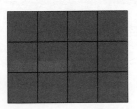

The rectangle has an area of 12 squares.

This rectangle is the same shape as an array. It has three rows of four squares. We can work out the area by working out three lots of four to get 12.

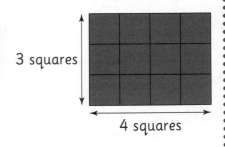

3 squares

4 squares

The area of a rectangle (or square) can be calculated by multiplying the number of rows by the number of squares in each row:

three rows of four squares makes 12 squares

3 × 4 squares = 12 squares

Let's practise

1) Describe the area of the shapes below and write the number story in your jotter (the first one has been done for you):

a)

three rows of three squares

$3 \times 3 = 9$

b)

c)

d)

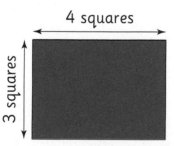

2) Write a number story to show how many blue squares would fit into each of these shapes.

a)

4 squares

3 squares

b)

2 squares

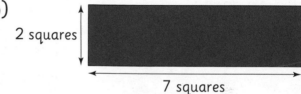

7 squares

⭐ **CHALLENGE!** . . . .

How many rectangles (or squares) can you draw that have an area of:

a) 16 squares   b) 24 squares

8.9 Area and arrays   155

9.1 Mathematicians and early number systems

> We are learning about early number systems.

Before we start

With a partner, discuss what a mathematician is. Can you name any famous mathematicians?

> A number system is a way to write and record numbers.

Let's learn

Here are some famous mathematicians:

Ada Lovelace *(born 1815):* She is now known as the first ever computer programmer.

Alan Turing *(born 1912):* He was a genius code-breaker and important in the theory of artificial intelligence.

Eukleidēs

Euclid *(born 365 BC):* Known for writing one of the very first mathematics textbooks.

Florence Nightingale *(born 1820):* Known for her work in nursing and the development of statistics.

Mathematicians usually work on number systems, which are a collection of things that represent and record quantities.

You can use tally marks to record quantities:

You can use dots to represent quantities:

Let's practise

1) Here is an image of the Chinese Mandarin number system. Work out what each symbol means.

一	二	三	四	五	六	七	八	九	十
十一	十二	十三	十四	十五	十六	十七	十八	十九	二十
二十一	二十二	二十三	二十四	二十五	二十六	二十七	二十八	二十九	三十

a) Write your age and today's date using Chinese Mandarin symbols.

b) With a partner, create your own number system to record the number of boys and girls in your class.

2) Investigate the famous mathematicians shown at the start of this unit. Can you find out more information – where they were born and how long they lived?

CHALLENGE!

Let's investigate...

With a partner, research different number systems.

How many can you name?

Now investigate more famous mathematicians and create a display about one that inspires you.

10.1 Continue number patterns and sequences

We are learning to recognise and continue number patterns and sequences.

Before we start

Fill in the missing element ? in these patterns:

a)

b)

Numbers can be **added**, **subtracted**, **multiplied or divided** to form a pattern or sequence.

Let's learn

Patterns and **sequences** can be made up by counting **forwards** and **backwards**.

Patterns and **sequences** can be created by using **multiplication or division**.

Look for familiar numbers and sequences in the following patterns.

You may have practised skip counting and multiplying for some of these patterns.

Let's practise

1) Write the missing numbers in each of these number patterns
   a) 4, 8, ☐ ? , 16, 20   b) 11, 22, ☐ ? , 44
   c) 21, 42, ☐ ? , 84   d) 18, 12, 6, ☐ ?

2) Continue each of these number patterns:
   a) 2, 4, 6, 8, …   b) 3, 6, 9, 12, …
   c) 15, 30, 45, …   d) 20, 17, 14, 11, …
   e) 25, 50, 75, 100, 125, …   f) 110, 100, 90, 80, 70, …

3) Write your own number pattern. Ask your partner to
   describe the rule. Take it in turns to do this.

CHALLENGE!

Isla has created some patterns involving numbers and shapes.
To make things more difficult for you, she has left some out.
What are the missing numbers or shapes?

a) 64, 32, 16, ☐ ? , 4   b) 15, ☐ ? , 45, 60, 75

c)

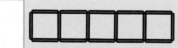
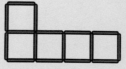
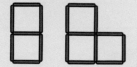

Try making the patterns using cubes, straws or counters.

10.2 Explain the rules for simple number sequences

We are learning to explain the rules for number sequences.

Before we start

Complete these number sequences:
a) 5, 10, 15, 20, ___?___, ___?___.
b) 16, 14, 12, 10, ___?___, ___?___.
c) 50, 60, 70, 80, ___?___, ___?___.

Number patterns and sequences can use **addition, subtraction, multiplication and division**.

Let's learn

To identify number patterns and sequences, you need to look at the starting number and then work out how much each number is **increasing** or **decreasing** by each time.

Let's practise

Resource
1C_10.2_Let's_Practise_Q1

1) Using the rule and the starting numbers provided, write the next five numbers for each pattern.

Rule	Starting number	First five terms				
Add 3	7	10	13	16		
Add 8	1					
Subtract 4	32					
Subtract 10	150					
Add 20	30					
Subtract 15	170					
Add 13	17					
Subtract 9	203					
Add 7	6					

2) Each row below shows a different number pattern. Look at each pattern in turn. What is the rule? When you have worked out the rule, write it down and use it to find the missing numbers in the gaps.

Resource 1C_10.2_Let's_Practise_Q2

First five terms					Rule
5	7	9	11	13	
25	21		13	9	
5	10	15		25	
23	31	39		55	

⭐ CHALLENGE!

a) Work with a partner to complete the following number pattern.

3, 8, [?], 18, 23, [?], 33

What do you notice about this number pattern?

Will 95 be in this pattern?

b) Will 37 be in this number pattern?

109, [?], 105, [?], 101

c) Will 99 be part of this number pattern?

2, [?], 6, [?], 10, 12

Write a pattern that will have 12 in it.
Challenge a partner to work out the rule.

11.1 Completing number sentences

We are learning to understand terms within a number sentence.

Before we start

Look at the following number statements and use 'true' or 'false' to answer:

a) $11 + 9 = 21$

b) $14 = 7 + 7$

c) $3 + 3 = 2 \times 3$

d) $30 - 10 = 12 + 7$

Equations are number sentences that always follow the same **pattern**.

Let's learn

Equations follow the same **pattern** and whatever comes before the equals sign (=) has the same value as what comes after it.

14 oranges + 7 oranges = 21 oranges

Both sides are **equal**.

Sometimes there is a missing number that you will have to find the value of.   **$10 + ? = 25$ $10 + 15 = 25$**

Let's practise

1) Copy and complete the following number sentences:

a) $8 + ? = 16$

b) $19 - ? = 5$

c) $? + 11 = 24$

d) $? - 6 = 13$

e) $12 \div ? = 6$

f) $? = 8 \times 2$

g) $40 = 4 \times ?$

h) $3 + 9 = 2 \times ?$

2) If ▲ = 5 and ● = 4, copy and complete the following equations:

a) i) $\boxed{?} + 6 = 10$

ii) $2 \times \boxed{?} = 10$

iii) $3 \times \boxed{?} = 15$

iv) $\boxed{?} - 1 = \boxed{?}$

b) If ▲ = + and ▲ = −, copy and complete the following equations:

i) $20 \boxed{?} 10 = 10$

ii) $5 \boxed{?} 8 = 13$

iii) $9 \boxed{?} 5 = 4$

iv) $6 \boxed{?} 6 = 14 \boxed{?} 2$

CHALLENGE!

1) Use these symbols to complete these number sentences. Some questions might have more than one possible answer!

greater than	>	less than	<
equal to	=	not equal to	≠

a) Forty-five $\boxed{?}$ Sixty-seven

b) $23 \boxed{?} 25 - 2$

c) $44 + 15 \boxed{?} 25 \times 3$

d) $24 \div 2 \boxed{?} 3 \times 4$

e) Thirty-five $\boxed{?}$ $\frac{1}{2}$ of seventy

f) Twelve add twenty $\boxed{?}$ Eighty divided by two

2) Now write four number sentences of your own.
Each number sentence must use a different symbol in it.
Ask a partner to check them.

12.1 Sorting 3D objects

We are learning to name and sort 3D objects.

Before we start

a) Amman has a 3D object in his pocket. 'It has one curved surface,' he says.

   What could his object be? Talk to a partner.

b) Isla has a 3D object with six faces.

   What could it be? Talk to a partner.

We can sort 3D objects by how many edges or vertices (corners) they have, or by the number or shapes of their faces.

Let's learn

Prisms have end faces that are exactly the same.

A triangular prism has six **vertices** and no curved faces. Its end faces are triangles.

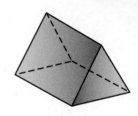

A hexagonal-based pyramid has seven vertices and no curved faces. Its base is a hexagon.

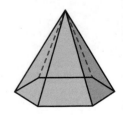

Let's practise

1) Complete each Venn diagram by writing the letter of the 3D object in the correct place.

a) A   B   C   D

At least one triangular face   D   At least one square face

b) E   F   G   H

At least one flat face   Has a curved face

2)

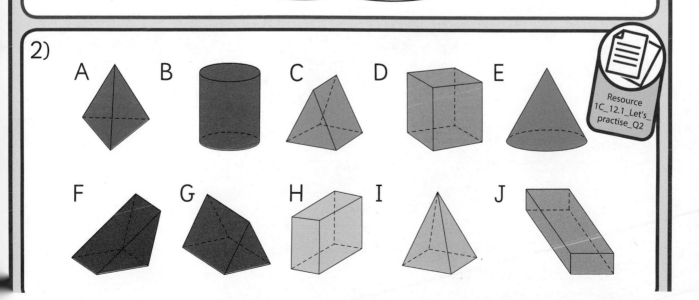

A   B   C   D   E

Resource 1C_12.1_Let's_practise_Q2

F   G   H   I   J

Copy and complete the table by writing the letter of each object in the correct place.

	Has a curved surface	Has three or more triangular faces	Has at least three rectangular faces
It is a prism			
It is not a prism			

3) Look at the 3D objects in question 2.

Write down the names of the objects that have:
a) four vertices   b) six vertices   c) eight edges
d) eight vertices   e) nine edges

⭐ **CHALLENGE!** ··································

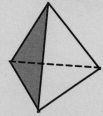 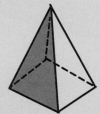 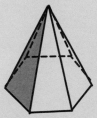 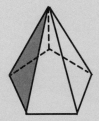 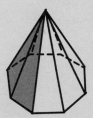

Resource 1C_12.1_Challenge

a) Copy and complete the table.

Pyramid base	Number of vertices at the base	Number of faces	Total number of vertices
Triangle	3	4	4
Square			
Pentagon			
Hexagon			
Octagon			

b) Predict how many faces there would be in a pyramid with a 10-sided shape as its base.

c) What about a pyramid with a 50-sided base?

12.2 Plan drawings

We are learning to identify 3D objects from plan drawings.

Before we start

Name these 3D objects and say what shape is found on their end face.

a)

b)

c)

When we look at 3D objects from different points of view, they look different.

Let's learn

We can look at a 3D object from the front, side or top. When we do this each view can look different!

Ask for some 3D shapes and try looking st one side at a time.

front view

side view

top view

plan view

1) Here are three cuboids. Match each cuboid to the plan views in the table by matching the letter of the cuboid to the number of the plan view.

A   B   C

	front view	side view	top view
1	◻	◻	◻
2	▭	▭	▭
3	▭	▭	▭

2) Name the 3D objects from their plan views.

	front view	side view	top view
a)	▭	▭	◯
b)	△	▭	▭
c)	◯	◯	◯

3) This table shows the side and plan views of three 3D objects. Name each object.

a)	Front view	Side view	plan view
b)	Front view	Side view	plan view
c)	Front view	Side view	plan view

⭐ **CHALLENGE!** ··

Here are the plan views of some 3D objects made from cubes.
a) Can you make the 3D objects using cubes?

	front view	side view	top view
a)			
b)			

Make your own 3D objects from cubes. Can you draw the front, side and top views?

12.3 Tiling patterns

> We are learning to make tiling patterns with more than one shape.

Before we start

Isla's grandad wants to tile his floor. Can he tile his floor with tiles that are this shape?

Explain your thinking.

> Some tiling patterns are made with more than one shape.

Let's learn

Some shapes will not tile by themselves.

A circle cannot tile by itself.

But a circle can tile with another shape. Here are two examples of tiling patterns where a circle is tiled with another shape.

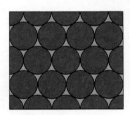

Let's practise

1) These floors all have patterns made with two tiles.

For each floor, draw the two shapes of the tiles that make the pattern.

a)

b)

c)
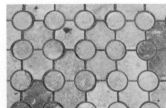

2) Make a tiling pattern by drawing round an octagon. What other shape do you need to make it tile?

3) Explore ways to make tiling patterns using these pairs of shapes. Can you find more than one way for each pair?

 You could make stencils out of cardboard.

a)

b)

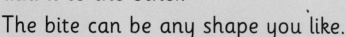

CHALLENGE!

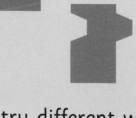

Draw any four-sided shape.

Now draw it again, only this time take a 'bite' out of one side and add it to the other.

The bite can be any shape you like.

This shape will tile, try it!

Start with a new four-sided shape and try different ways of taking 'bites'. Again, try to tile the shape.

What if you add the bite so it is higher or lower than where you took it from?

What if you add the bite to an adjacent side instead of an opposite one?

What happens if you take more than one bite?

Will the shape still tile?

13.1 Identifying angles

We are learning to identify angles that are bigger or smaller than a right angle.

Before we start

List three objects that contain right angles.

Angles are a measurement of turn.

Let's learn

A right-angle tester measures 90°. It is used to compare angles and to test whether the size of the angle is less than or more than a right angle.

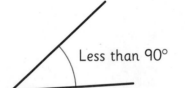
Less than 90°

More than 90°

Let's practise

1) Use your right-angle tester.

   Write the letters of the pizza slices that show an angle:
   a) less than a right angle   b) more than a right angle

   A   B   C

   D   E    F

2) A bee flew from flower to flower to collect pollen.

Test the amount of turn the bee made each time.

Write 'less than a quarter turn' or 'more than a quarter turn' next to each letter in your jotter.

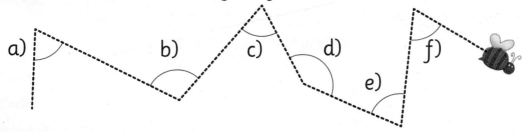

a)   b)   c)   d)   f)

e)

3) Test the size of each angle with your right-angle tester.
Complete the table below. Write the letter of each angle in the correct column.

About 90°	Less than 90°	More than 90°

a)   b)   c)   d)

e)   f)   g)   h)

CHALLENGE!

Amman says 'my shape has two right angles, one angle that is bigger than a right angle and one angle that is smaller than a right angle.'

Draw Amman's shape.

What is the name of this shape?

13.2 Half and quarter turns

We are learning to describe half and quarter turns in degrees.

Before we start

The square is turned either a quarter or a half turn. The turned squares are put into a grid.

One of the squares is not right.

Write down the grid reference of the wrong square.

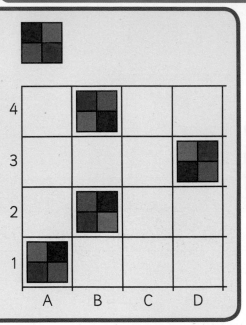

A quarter turn measures 90 degrees. A half turn is two quarter turns. It measures 180 degrees.

Let's learn

Nuria is writing direction code for Finlay.

To follow the route, Finlay must:

Go forward 3, turn right 90 degrees, go forward 2, turn left 90 degrees, go forward 1.

Try programming online with the Logo coding system.

Nuria writes:

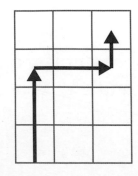

Forward 3
Right 90
Forward 2
Left 90
Forward 1

1) Amman is jumping on stepping stones. This is the route he takes:

   Copy and complete these directions for Amman's route:

   Forward 1

   Left 90

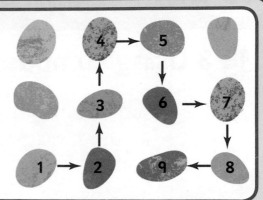

2) Programme the robot to travel the route in red, by completing the directions:

   Forward 2

   Left 90 ...

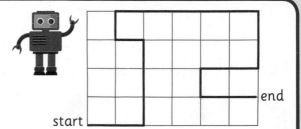

start   end

3) Isla is standing in D3, facing D1 and D2.

   She follows these directions:

   Backward 2 > Right 90 > Forward 3 > Left 90 > Forward 2 > Right 90 > Backward 1 > Left 90 > Forward 2 > Left 90 > Forward 1 > Left 90 > Forward 3 > Right 180 > Forward 2 > Left 90 > Forward 2

   Which square does Isla end up in?

Resource 1C_13.2_Let's practise_Q3

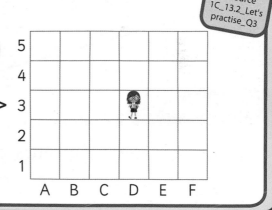

A B C D E F

CHALLENGE!

Work with a partner.

Use a grid like the one in question 3.

Choose a starting point and draw a route.

Without showing them, describe your route to your partner.

Have they ended up on the correct square?

13.3 Using compass points

> We are learning to give and follow directions using the points of the compass.

Before we start

Which of these shows this ring after a quarter turn anti-clockwise?

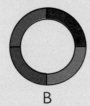 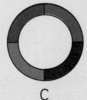 

A   B   C

> A compass contains a magnet, which lines up with the Earth's magnetic field so that it always points north.

Let's learn

Because it always points north, a compass is used to find the direction of places.

A compass shows these points: north, south, east and west.

They can be written N, S, E and W.

North

The red arrow on a compass always points north.

You have to turn the compass to make the red arrow line up with **N**.

 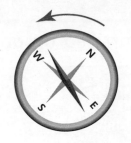

Let's practise

1)

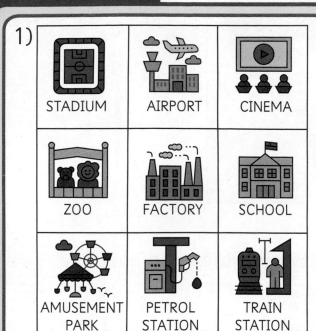

a) You are at the factory. Write down the name of the place that is to the
   i) north   ii) south   iii) east   iv) west of the factory

b) Write which place is
   i)   north of the zoo
   ii) west of the cinema
   iii) east of the amusement park
   iv) south of the stadium
   v)   east of the airport
   vi) west of the petrol station

2) You have arrived on an exotic island.

Resource 1C_13.3_Let's practise_Q2

Follow these directions.

a) Start at the rock. Go north two squares and east one square. Write where you think you are now in your jotter.

b) Start at the volcano. Go south three squares and west one square. Write where you think you are now in your jotter.

c) Start at the cactus. Go south one square and east three squares. Write where you think you are now in your jotter.

d) Start at the rock. Go north four squares, west one square and south two squares. Write where you think you are now in your jotter.

3)

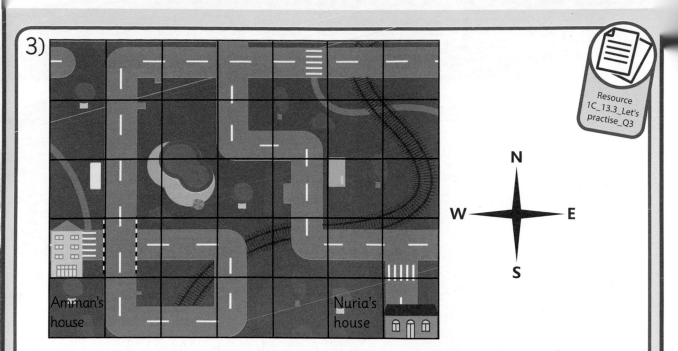

a) Copy and complete the directions to get from Nuria's house to Amman's house by road (the black and white dotted line shows a bridge – you must go straight over or underneath):

Go one square north, two squares west …

b) Write directions to go back to Nuria's house from Amman's house.

Resource
1C_13.3_Let's
practise_Q3

Resource 1C_
13.3_Challenge

CHALLENGE!

Finlay is trapped on an alien planet, with poisonous alien plants which he must avoid.

How many different sets of directions can you write to help Finlay escape unharmed? You must not go back over your steps!

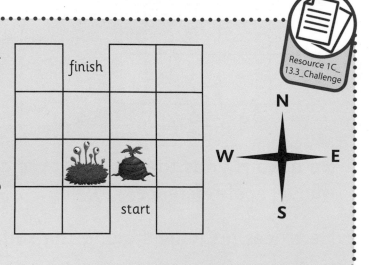

13.4 Grid references

We are learning to read and plot two figure grid references.

Before we start

Finlay says the pentagon is at C2.
Isla says it is at 2C.

Who is right? Explain your answer.

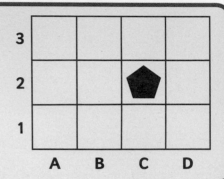

The horizontal grid reference comes first; the vertical reference is second.

Let's learn

Finlay is plotting two-figure grid references.

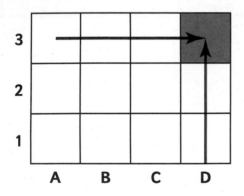

He always finds the horizontal reference first. Then he finds the vertical reference.

He traces his fingers along the squares until they meet.

He colours the square where his fingers meet.

1) Copy this grid into your jotter.

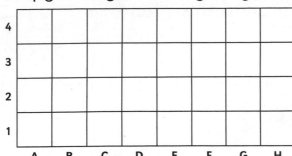

Resource 1C_13.4_Let's_practise_Q1

Plot the following grid references by colouring the squares:

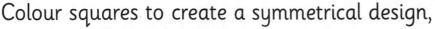
B4 - G3 - A2 - F4 - A4 - B2 - D2 - H4 - D1 - A3 - D3 - G1 - G2 - A1 - G4 - D4

What word have you made?

2) Work with a partner.

Copy this grid into your jotter.

Colour squares to create a symmetrical design, using two or three colours.

Do not colour every square.

Keeping your design hidden, tell your partner which squares to colour, using grid references.

Can they make your design?

Swap roles.

 Colour A5 red.

Resource 1C_13.4_Let's_practise_Q2

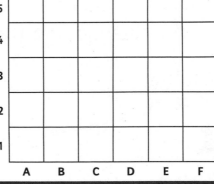

3) Use the grid from question 2.

Imagine you are standing in these squares, facing north.

a) Write down these grid references:

   i) Start at B5. Go three squares east.

   ii) Start at E1. Go two squares west.

   iii) Start at E3. Go two squares north and one square east

   iv) Start at A1. Go three squares north, three squares east, one square south.

   v) Start at F5. Go four squares south and two squares west.

b) Copy the grid into your jotter and colour the grid references you found.

CHALLENGE!

Pirates have buried treasure all around this island.

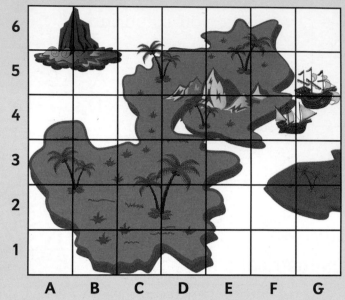

a) Follow the clues to find the places where the treasure can be found:

   i)   The first treasure chest is buried at D5.

   ii) The second treasure chest is buried two squares south of the first chest. Write the grid reference in your jotter.

   iii) The third chest is buried three squares west and one square south of the second chest. Write the grid reference in your jotter.

   iv) The fourth chest is buried two squares east and three squares north of the third chest. Write the grid reference in your jotter.

   v) The fifth chest is buried three squares east and one square north of the fourth chest. Write the grid reference in your jotter.

b) Copy the grid (you don't need to copy the map) and plot the places where the treasure is buried.

13.5 Symmetry

We are learning to create symmetrical designs with more than one line of symmetry.

Before we start

Which shape is not symmetrical?

A  B C D

Some things have more than one line of symmetry.

Let's learn

A rectangle has two lines of symmetry.
It still looks like a rectangle when you put a mirror on it this way:

 or this way:

Let's practise

1) Take a piece of paper. Fold it in half then fold it in half again the other way.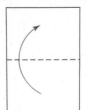

Use scissors to cut shapes out from the edges of your folded-up piece of paper.

Unfold your paper. You should now have a design with two lines of symmetry. Ask a partner to check it is symmetrical.

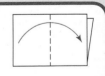

2) Draw a mirror line. Use cubes, tiles or other objects to make a symmetrical design.

Now draw another mirror line, and copy the design so that it is symmetrical in the new mirror line.

Make two designs of your own and take a photo or draw a picture of the finished design.

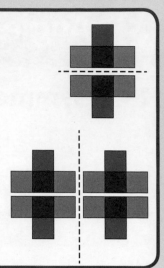

3) Isla has a crate that holds 16 bottles. She has four bottles of water, eight bottles of milk and four bottles of orange juice. How many different ways can you arrange the bottles into the crate so that it is symmetrical in both mirror lines?

Use counters to help you.

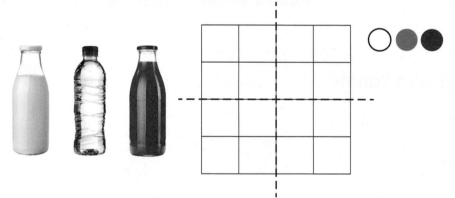

CHALLENGE!

Find examples of symmetry in the environment. Take photographs if possible.

Can you find examples of objects or things that have more than one line of symmetry?

14 Data handling and analysis

14.1 Collect, organise and display data

We are learning to collect, organise and display.

Before we start

Find out what month has the most birthdays in your class.

- Record the information using tally marks.
- Display the results in a bar chart.

Information can be collected by creating a **survey** and asking **questions**.

Let's learn

We use surveys to collect information.

This is an example of an open-ended survey question.

'*What is your favourite colour?*'

The person can respond in any way they wish.

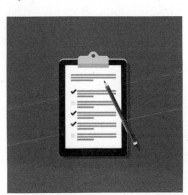

This is an example of a closed-ended survey question.

'*What is your favourite colour: red, blue, yellow or green?*'

The person has to choose from the options given.

Many surveys use closed-ended questions because the data is easier to count.

1) Tick the correct question type.

Question	Closed-ended	Open-ended
Which animal do you prefer, cats or rabbits?		
What is your favourite TV programme?		
Which fruit do you like the best?		
What is your favourite sport, football or tennis?		
How many brothers and sisters do you have?		
How many books have you read this week, one, two or three?		

CHALLENGE!

Finlay wants to find out the favourite colours of students in his class.

Design a recording sheet or table for Finlay to collect the information.

If you know how to use tally marks, you could use a tally table.

Now design your own recording sheet on a piece of paper to find out the favourite colours of students in your class. Go around the class and record the information as you find it out.

Now show your results in a chart or diagram.

14.2 Use data to create Carroll and Venn diagrams

> We are learning to use data to create Carroll and Venn diagrams.

Before we start

Work with a partner to complete the following table:

How do pupils travel to school?	Tally
Bus	
Cycle	
Car	
Walk	
Total	

> Information can be displayed by creating Carroll and Venn diagrams.

Let's learn

A **Carroll diagram** is used to organise data and group it.

	Shapes with curved lines	Shapes with straight lines
Three or fewer sides	●	▲
More than three sides	⬣	■

A **Venn diagram** shows the relationship between a group of different things.

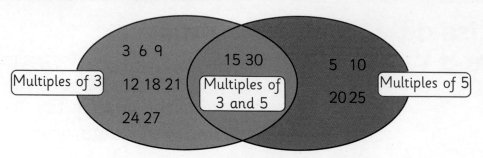

Let's practise

1) Copy and complete the following Carroll diagram:

	Vegetable	Fruit
Green		
Not green		

2) Copy and complete the following Venn diagram:

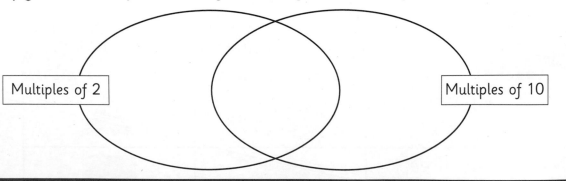

Multiples of 2   Multiples of 10

Copy and complete the following Carroll diagram by asking your class if they have any cats or dogs.

	Cats	No cats
Dogs		
No dogs		

In your class what is the most common situation?

· People with dogs and cats.

· People with dogs and no cats.

· People with cats and no dogs.

· People with no cats and no dogs.

Try to create a Venn diagram to display your results:

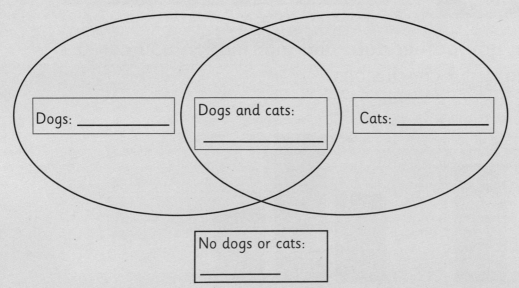

Dogs: _____

Dogs and cats: _____

Cats: _____

No dogs or cats: _____

14.3 Use data to check and verify information

> We are learning to use data to check and verify information.

Before we start

Look at the table and discuss with a partner what the data tells you.

Colour	Number of students (tally marks)
Red	⠀卌 ⦀⦀⦀
Blue	卌
Green	⦀⦀⦀
Yellow	卌
Purple	⎮

> Use information that you gather to draw conclusions.

Let's learn

When you gather data and information you can use this to draw conclusions.

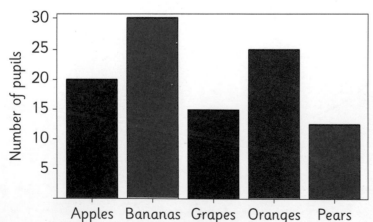

From the data on the chart we know that:

- Bananas are the most popular fruit

- Pears are the least popular fruit

- 25 pupils prefer oranges

- 15 pupils like grapes

Let's practise

1) Copy and complete the table.

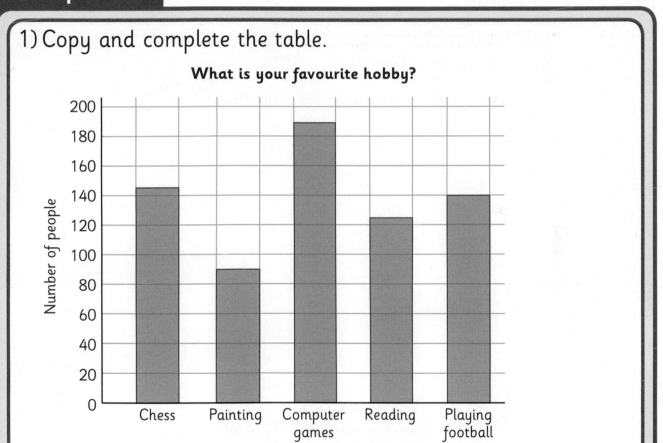

What is your favourite hobby?

Statement	True	False
'I notice that chess is more popular than painting.'		
'I notice that three of the bars are close to the same height, and that one bar is a lot smaller.'		
'I notice that the least popular hobby is reading.'		
'I notice that computer games are over three times more popular than painting.'		
'I notice that the most popular hobby is computer games.'		

2) Copy and complete the table.

Height of a bean plant over eight weeks

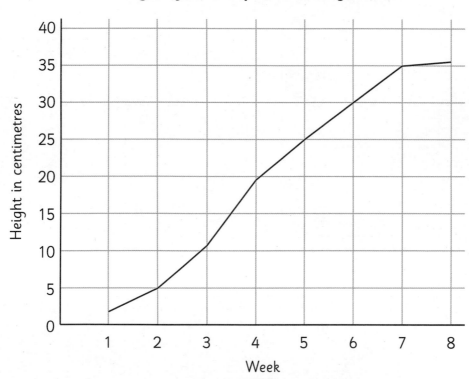

Data handling and analysis

Statement	True	False
'I notice that the line goes up and then begins to level out at the end.'		
'I notice that the bean plant reaches a height of nearly 45 cm by week 8.'		
'I notice that in week 6 the bean plant has grown to just over 30 cm.'		
'I notice that the bean plant is almost three times as large in week 6 as it is in week 4.'		

CHALLENGE!

Look at the bean plant graph again.
Use information from the graph to copy and complete the statements.

1) I notice that the line goes up for most of the graph.

   This means...

2) I notice that the line starts to level out after week 7.

   This means...

3) I notice that between weeks 1 and 7 the line goes up by a similar amount each week.
   This means...

4) Write three 'I notice statements' for the data you are working with in your statistical inquiry.

14.4 Solve problems using data, graphs and diagrams

> We are learning to solve problems using data, graphs and diagrams.

Before we start

The double bar graph shows the number of laptops sold by two computer shops. Answer the questions that follow.

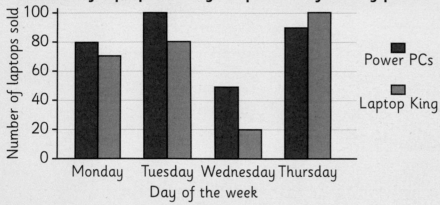

Number of laptops sold by shops over a four-day period

a) Laptop King sold how many laptops on Thursday?

b) What day of the week showed the biggest difference in sales between the two companies?

c) Power PCs sold how many more laptops than Laptop King on Wednesday?

> Use data, graphs and diagrams to solve problems.

Let's learn

Different types of graphs, such as double bar, double line and 3D graphs, can tell us different things. Look at all the information to draw conclusions.

1) Match the table to the correct picture graph.

Resource
1C_14.4_Let's
practise_Q1

a)

Fruit	Number of people (tally marks)
Apple	卌卌 I
Orange	卌卌 II
Banana	卌 II
Mango	卌 III

b)

Fruit	Number of people (frequency)
Apple	9
Orange	12
Banana	11
Mango	8

c)

Fruit	Number of people (tally marks)
Apple	卌卌卌 I
Orange	卌卌 I
Banana	卌 II
Mango	卌 III

d) Number of people who like a particular fruit   ● = 2

Apple   Orange   Banana   Mango

e) Number of people
who like a particular
fruit ● = 2

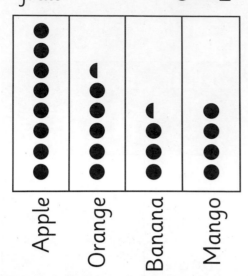

f) Number of people
who like a particular
fruit ● = 2

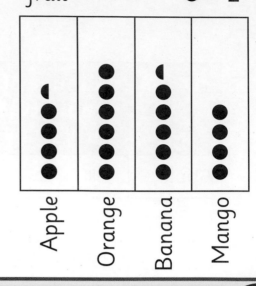

2) i) Draw a circle around the table or graph that
is the odd one out.

ii) Discuss with a partner why you think it is the
odd one out.

Resource 1C_
14.4_Let's
practise_Q2

a)

Ice-cream flavour	Number of people (tally marks)
Cherry	卌 卌 卌 II
Toffee	卌 II
Banana	卌 卌 II
Chocolate	卌 卌 I

b) **Number of people who like a particular flavour of ice-cream** ○ = 2

Data handling and analysis

Several bars of data are missing from the bar graph below. Use the information in the pie charts to add the missing information to the bar graph.

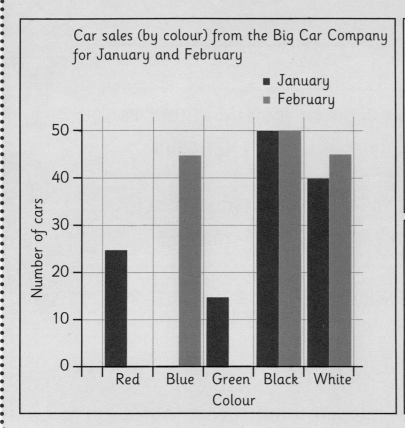

Car sales (by colour) from the Big Car Company for January and February

■ January
■ February

Number of cars / Colour
Red, Blue, Green, Black, White

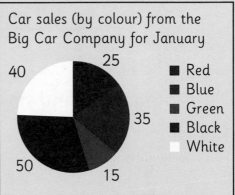

Car sales (by colour) from the Big Car Company for January

25
40
35
50
15

■ Red
■ Blue
■ Green
■ Black
■ White

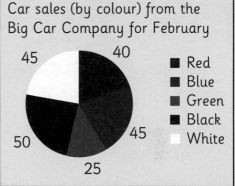

Car sales (by colour) from the Big Car Company for February

45
40
45
50
25

■ Red
■ Blue
■ Green
■ Black
■ White

15.1 Using data to predict the outcome

We are learning to use data to predict the outcome of everyday events.

Before we start

With a partner, find an example of something that is:

Certain   Possible   Impossible

Things can be **certain**, **possible**, **unlikely** or **impossible**.

Let's learn

The questions on these pages are all to do with choosing whether an event will not happen, could happen or will happen.

For example:

Something that **will not** happen tomorrow is that a horse will start school in your class.

Something that **will** happen tomorrow is that during the daytime it will be light.

Something that **could** happen tomorrow is that you could hear a really funny joke.

We use the following words to describe the chance of something happening:

- **Impossible** — it will never happen
- **Unlikely** — it may happen but probably will not
- **Likely** — it may happen and probably will
- **Certain** — it will definitely happen

Events can be placed on a **probability scale** to show the chances of them happening:

Impossible **Unlikely** **Possible** **Certain**

Let's practise

1) Draw something that will not happen and something that will happen tomorrow.

2) Scottish Weather TV have asked for your help with their weather report. Decide whether each event will not happen, could happen or will happen and then match them to the correct words.

a) On Monday it will rain cheese.

b) On Tuesday the sky will be above your head.

c) On Wednesday it will be warm.

d) On Thursday there will be thunder that sounds like a chicken.

e) On Friday it will be windy.

Will not happen

Could happen

Will happen

3) Look carefully at this school timetable. Choose whether you think the event will not, could or will happen.

Sunday	Monday	Tuesday	Wednesday	Thursday
You will drink something.	A tree will grow through your classroom floor.	You will drop your pencil on the floor.	There will be a 'Bring Your Pet Elephant To School' day.	You will be praised for your hard work.

Copy and complete these statements, explaining why you have made your choices.

a) I think that Sunday's event will not / could / will happen because...

b) I think that Monday's event will not / could / will happen because...

c) I think that Tuesday's event will not / could / will happen because...

d) I think that Wednesday's event will not / could / will happen because...

e) I think that Thursday's event will not / could / will happen because...

CHALLENGE!

Work with a partner. Mix up 10 red counters and 10 blue counters under your jotters. Each partner should take it in turns to close their eyes and pick 10 counters. Do this 5 times each and write down your results. Now discuss the following statements and say if they are impossible, possible or certain to happen.

Partner A picks all the red counters and partner B picks all the blue counters.

Partner A picks orange counters.

Partner A and B both pick the same number of red and blue counters.

Partner A and B pick 10 counters each.

Ideas of chance and uncertainty